PREACHING
MATTHEW

*To James Hines—our former dean who
encouraged us to team-teach the gospel of
Matthew, and whose life is good news indeed!*

PREACHING MATTHEW

Interpretation and Proclamation

MIKE GRAVES
DAVID M. MAY

CHALICE
PRESS

ST. LOUIS, MISSOURI

Bible quotations, unless otherwise noted, are from the *New Revised Standard Version Bible,* copyright 1989, Division of Christian Education of the National Council of the Churches of Christ in the United States of America. Used by permission. All rights reserved.

Cover art: © The Crosiers
Cover and interior design: Elizabeth Wright

Visit Chalice Press on the World Wide Web at
www.chalicepress.com

10 9 8 7 6 5 4 3 2 1   07 08 09 10 11 12

Library of Congress Cataloging–in–Publication Data

May, David M.
  Preaching Matthew : interpretation and proclamation / David May and Mike Graves.
    p. cm.
  ISBN 978-0-8272-3005-7
  1. Bible. N.T. Matthew—Sermons. 2. Bible. N.T. Matthew—Criticism, interpretation, etc. I. Graves, Mike. II. Title.
  BS2575.54.M39 2008
  226.2'06—dc22
                              2007037169

Printed in the United States of America

Contents

Acknowledgments

The majority of New Testament scholars believe the writer of Matthew's gospel had a copy of Mark in front of him and drew on it heavily at times. Likewise, we stand on the shoulders of many scholars, but many others as well—persons who supported us in the writing of this volume. We are especially grateful to former Chalice Press editor, Jon Berquist, who originally entrusted this project to us. We think also of Jane McAvoy, who encouraged this project along before her untimely death. More recently, Trent Butler demonstrated remarkable patience with a project that got stalled along the way at many junctures. Many thanks, then, to the staff of Chalice Press and their commitment to books for preachers.

Other communities have sustained us over the years. First, those who taught us the Bible and Greek in our seminary experience: Gerald Borchert and Sharon Gritz, as well as our teachers through books, John Pilch and Bruce J. Malina. We also wish to express gratitude to our seminary families, the folks of Central Baptist Theological Seminary, and—more recently for one of us—Saint Paul School of Theology. Lastly, we give thanks for our families—our parents, spouses, children (in the case of one of us), as well as animal companions (in the case of both of us)—for their unending love and support. Thanks be to God.

Introduction

"One does not live by bread alone,
but by every word that comes from the mouth of God."

MATTHEW 4:4

"Now, those who read the scriptures must not only them-
selves understand them, but must also as lovers of learning
be able through the spoken and written word to help the
outsiders."

THE PROLOGUE OF SIRACH

Our Focus

When the late Igor Kipnis died, the classical music world lost one of its great modern harpsichordists. Kipnis, who loved to play the relatively unknown and archaic instrument, also enjoyed introducing it to others. He noted that most folks, if they even know what a harpsichord is, picture a scene from eighteenth-century Vienna, court musicians in powdered wigs, arrayed in strange clothes. As for the instrument itself, he said, people expect to find it in some dusty attic. In an interview on National Public Radio, Kipnis added, "That's all right. I either bring it down from the attic or invite them up."

Some churchgoers feel the same way about the Bible, as if the characters on its pages are not real, their clothes and customs coming from a far-off fantasy land. Such people think that the texts themselves belong in a trunk up in the attic. Take, for example, the story Harvey Cox tells, about a woman who tried to call Jerusalem from a city in the southwestern part of the United States, only to be told by the operator, "Jerusalem isn't a *real* city, honey, it's only in the Bible!"[1] People are constantly misunderstanding texts from the Bible, and the gospel of Matthew is no exception. As preachers, however, we know better! Thus, like Kipnis, we are given the privileged task of introducing folks to the ancient story, removing it from the attic and bringing it out to the main streets of our modern cities, towns, and villages.

Two great hopes sustain the writing of this book. The first is our belief that Scripture had a transforming influence on our ancestors in faith, and that similar transforming experiences can still be captured for listeners today by way of Scripture.[2] The second hope is that this book contains fresh approaches for preaching the gospel of Matthew so that when used along with other available resources, it will spark your thinking.

Our Approach

We base our approach on two deceptively simple words: *what* and *how*. *What* refers to the interpretive work necessary for sermon preparation; *how* to the homiletical issues the various text-segments raise. Of course, these processes are nothing new to preachers. Week in and week out, we wrestle with *what* passages of Scripture mean and *how* we will communicate this to our listeners. Although a familiar scenario, according to Fred Craddock, it is also "fundamental to the task of sermon preparation." He writes, "The process of arriving at something to say is to be distinguished from the process of determining how to say it... Unless the minister has two eurekas, it is not likely the listeners will have one."[3]

These two simple but important words, *what* and *how*, give shape to what we call a "socio-rhetorical homiletic." Rather than "let the reader understand," allow us to explain what we mean. As interpreters of the ancient text, we are called to be sensitive to the *social* norms and values of the first-century world. New Testament scholar Bruce Malina has succinctly described the importance of this step by noting that "readings produced with no thought to being considerate of what the authors...meant in their original time, place and culture are, as a rule, unethical readings."[4] To be a considerate reader, "The task of a contemporary preacher or teacher is to read and hear the [narratives], as near as possible, with the same ears and eyes as the first readers and listeners."[5]

The *rhetorical* dimension demands that we also pay close attention to the literary form of the passage before us, the shape in which the evangelist has written the story. As C. Clifton Black notes, the New Testament writers were artists, "creatively fusing form and content."[6] Unfortunately, as Thomas Long observes, while preachers frequently think about "images, plots, arguments, and poetic devices, as they appear within *sermons,* there is not much help about what sense or use to make of those very same elements when they appear in the *texts* from which those sermons spring."[7] When we read a passage given in parable form, for instance, we instinctively know as interpreters that the rules are different than when reading a miracle story. Those "rules" also apply to preaching, a recognition increasingly more appreciated by biblical scholars and homileticians alike.[8]

Of course, while the process of sermon preparation always begins with interpretation, it can never end there. Thus the need exists for a *homiletical* focus as well, a homiletic that accounts for the sociological and rhetorical dimensions of interpretation and presentation. In preaching, as in music, more is involved than simply explaining what something meant or means. Instruments must be played, and in a sense so must texts and sermons. When Sunday comes, we preachers know that more is needed than just a report on *what* the text means; *how* we say it matters as well. As Saint Augustine, the church's first homiletician, put it, in addition to "moving" people to respond, sermons must "teach and delight."[9] In other words, biblical preaching is not only preaching *from* the Bible but learning from the Bible *how* to preach.

With that in mind, we propose that two sets of questions be asked of each text-segment when preparing to preach, questions we used to organize our thoughts on Matthew's gospel:

The *What* Questions ————————————————

THEN	**Now**
What meaning(s) might Matthew's community have heard in this passage?	*What meaning(s) might the passage have for our community today?*

The *How* Questions ————————————————

THEN	**Now**
How did the evangelist, using ancient literary conventions, craft the passage?	*How shall we, using homiletical wisdom, craft our sermon?*

In addition to these questions, for each passage examined we offer sermon excerpts and/or whole sermons. With each text-segment, readers are invited into two conversations, one with the text and a biblical scholar, the other with a sermon and a homiletician. Some preachers will find it helpful to read the exegetical material only after meditating on the text-segment; others will want to dive in right away. Still others may find it helpful to consider even the homiletical material early on in the process. Not everyone follows the same path to sermon preparation.

Those who are familiar with Matthew's presence in Year A of the Revised Common Lectionary will readily note that not every text-segment is included here. The genealogy of Jesus, for instance, is not included, which is a shame, since Matthew included the names of Gentile women in the listing. The same is true for the feeding of the multitudes, of which Matthew includes two versions. We did attempt, however, to capture the essence of Matthew's overall plot (infancy, major motifs of his ministry, and resurrection), while including a diversity of literary forms (parables as well as pronouncement stories, and so forth).

As with most scholarly endeavors, we stand on the shoulders of those who have gone before, that "great cloud of witnesses" and the testimonies they have left behind in the form of commentaries. Fortunately, no longer must preachers wade through dusty tomes filled with esoteric facts, or settle for "Simple Sermon Outlines for Sunday" or some such nonsense. Several fine resources are available today, commentaries written with one eye on the text and the other on the pulpit.[10] We are grateful for their contributions, and hopeful that ours will prove helpful as well.

Our Hope

In the final analysis, what we hope for is the same thing all preachers hope for, the same thing the evangelist hoped for when he first penned his message. If it helps, think of Matthew's gospel as an extended narrative sermon for his faith community some fifty years or so removed from the Christ event. He tells them the story, *the Story,* hoping that his readers/listeners will find themselves in the tale, that the news of Jesus' resurrection from the dead will affect readers years later the same way it did those believers in first-century Palestine. What more could a preacher ask for?

Additional Resources

The following resources are some of the more helpful commentaries preachers might wish to consider when preaching from Matthew:

Eugene M. Boring, *Matthew* in *New Interpreter's Bible,* vol. 8 (Nashville: Abingdon Press, 1995).

Warren Carter, *Matthew and the Margins: A Sociopolitical and Religious Reading* (Maryknoll, N.Y.: Orbis, 2001).

D. Garland, *Reading Matthew: A Literary and Theological Commentary on the First Gospel* (New York: Crossroad, 1995).

Douglas R.A. Hare, *Matthew* in *Interpretation* (Louisville: John Knox Press, 1993).

Richard A. Jensen, *Preaching Matthew's Gospel* (Lima, Ohio: CSS, 1998).

Thomas G. Long, *Matthew* in *Westminster Bible Companion* (Louisville: Westminster John Knox Press, 1997).

Eduard Schweizer, *The Good News According to Matthew,* trans. David E. Green (Atlanta: John Knox Press, 1975).

CHAPTER 1

Matthew 2:13–23

Jesus' Journey to Egypt

Locating the Sermon

First Sunday after Christmas (Year A)

If the soundtrack for Luke's better-known Christmas pageant is "Silent Night, Holy Night," then imagine what kind of music might accompany this story in Matthew's gospel. Coming on the heels of Lessons and Carols services in candlelit sanctuaries, with families gathering around fireplaces and the singing of Handel's *Messiah* echoing, it is not surprising that many preachers prefer the annual Epiphany reading from Matthew 2:1–12, about visitors from the East bearing gifts and warnings, over this story about the "slaughter of the innocents" and Jesus' narrow escape. But as every family knows, ancient as well as modern, life is sometimes hellish. Preachers will have no trouble finding examples of injustice, locally or globally, with which to connect this biblical story. Of course, we must start with the ancient story.

Understanding the Passage

This text-segment stands at a strategic place in the Matthean birth narrative because it represents the last word Matthew[1] wrote about the events surrounding Jesus' birth. This account began in 1:1 with the recounting of Jesus' honorable and royal Davidic origins. It will end with a clash between dynasties, the Herodian and the Davidian. From Matthew's perspective, this clash represents a contrast between the temporal and fading Herodian dynasty, which still could wield a bloody sword, and the ascending Davidic kingship, an everlasting spiritual dynasty that sprang from an unremarkable and unlikely place—a house in Bethlehem. With a deft and artistic stroke, the author captures the clash between these two kingdoms. Also within the birth narrative, Matthew creates for listeners a sense of the always-affirming guidance of God's providence.

How the Evangelist Crafted the Text-segment

In this passage Matthew presents a very balanced composition. He has used a technique called a "chiasm."[2] In a typical chiasm a text-segment has a balanced composition of outside stories paralleling one another as they move toward the center of the text-segment: A^1, B^1, C, B^2, A^2. This reverse parallelism creates a "sandwich effect" in which an author draws particular attention to important elements within the pivotal center. Very much like the Greek letter Xi (x) for which this technique is named, X marks the spot for what is most significant. Verses 13–15 represent the first part of the chiasm, i.e., leaving Israel and traveling to Egypt, while verses 19–23 represent the second reversing parallelism, i.e., leaving Egypt and traveling to Israel. Note some of the connecting elements between these two parts of the story. Both verse 13 and verse 19 begin with an angel of the Lord and a dream given to Joseph. Each has instructions about taking the child and traveling. Both sections end with a prophetic citation from the Hebrew Scriptures, verse 15 and verse 23, respectively. Perhaps it helps to see the arrangement within the text-segment itself as laid out below.

13 Now after they left,

> an angel of the Lord appeared to Joseph in a dream and said,
>> "Get up, take the child and his mother, and flee to Egypt,
>> and remain there until I tell you; for Herod is about to search
>> for the child, to destroy him."
>>> 14 Then Joseph
>>>> *got up, took the child and his mother by night, and went to Egypt,*
>>>>> 15 and remained there until the death of Herod.
>>>>>> This was to fulfill what had been spoken by
>>>>>> the Lord through the prophet,
>>>>>>> "Out of Egypt I have called my son."

16 When Herod saw that he had been tricked by the wise men, he was infuriated, and he sent and killed all children in and around Bethlehem who were two years old or under, according to the time that he had learned from the wise men. 17 Then was fulfilled what had been spoken through the prophet Jeremiah: 18 "A voice was heard in Ramah, wailing and loud lamentation, Rachel weeping for her children; she refuses to be consoled, because they are no more."

>>> 19 When Herod died,
>>>> an angel of the Lord suddenly appeared in a dream to
>>>> Joseph in Egypt and said,
>>> 20 "Get up, take the child and his mother, and go to the land
>>> of Israel, for those who were seeking the child's life are dead."
>>> 21 Then Joseph
>> *got up, took the child and his mother, and went to the land of Israel.*
>> 22 But when he heard that Archelaus was ruling over Judea in place
>> of his father Herod, he was afraid to go there. After being warned in a
>> dream, he went away to the district of Galilee. 23 There he made his
>> home in a town called Nazareth,

so that what had been spoken through the prophets might be fulfilled,
"He will be called a Nazorean."

If the Egyptian flight and return represent parallel frames, then Matthew may be directing the listener's attention to the significance of the picture they surround. The picture Matthew presents as the pivotal focus is the killing of all the male children two years or younger in Bethlehem and the vicinity, an event traditionally called the "Slaughter of the Innocents." One point of connection that this interior story (set off in bold in example) has to the exterior stories is that it also ends with a citation from the Hebrew Scriptures.

This tendency by Matthew to use the Hebrew Scriptures illustrates another technique he likes to employ—the "fulfill-ment motif." Matthew illustrates for his listeners that events in the recent past, i.e., Jesus' birth, have connection by way of the prophets' words with the distant past of Israel's history. The connection represented by the words of the prophet illustrates God's continued covenant faithfulness to God's people. Granted, this faithfulness is found in the most unusual circumstance, i.e., in a vulnerable child from an oppressed people, in a backwater village of a third-rate province.

The Matthean fulfillment passages also generate echoes. By citation of particular passages, Matthew is not just trying to "prove" an event was foretold, but he is attempting to get the reader to hear the echoes from previous stories. What is important is not just the specific passage from the Hebrew Scriptures but the whole narrative in which the passage is found.

The verses highlighting fulfillment (vv. 15, 17–18, and 23) follow a typical pattern: "this was to fulfill what had been spoken by the Lord through the prophet," and then a passage from the Hebrew Scriptures is cited. Verse 15, "Out of Egypt have I called my son," is from the prophet Hosea, 11:1. Egypt was not only a place of sanctuary, but also that place of origin for the greatest of all liberators in Israel's history, Moses. As this passage is heard, it sends echoes through its listeners about Egypt and Moses, reminding the Judeans of God's faithfulness in the past even in the midst of oppression and bondage. To hear about rising *at night* and fleeing to freedom and safety in Egypt must have stirred deep irony in the original listeners. Their ancestors had fled Egypt *at night* for the freedom and safety of the promised land (Israel). The Egypt/son reference was also a way in which Jesus was explicitly compared to Moses, who also had to deal with violent, oppressive power (that of the Pharaohic dynasty) from birth through adulthood.

As noted above, Matthew apparently places special significance on this interior story, verses 16–18, a most painful story in an otherwise hopeful and joyous narrative. This painful narrative finds its climax in the fulfillment formula of verses 17—18, which deal with a quote taken from the prophet Jeremiah, 31:15. The background for this fulfillment passage is the Babylonian invasion and destruction of Judah in 587 B.C.E., the beginning of exile for the nation of Israel. Matthew has symbolized that Jesus and his family also experience exile. But even more than just Joseph's clan, the village of Bethlehem is in exile without a future because the sons of Israel, a family's hope, have been killed.

While the citation from Jeremiah seems to echo with the intensity of pain and hopelessness, a small reverberation of hope echoes within the weeping. For while Matthew is citing a reference from the prophet Jeremiah, Jeremiah is actually referring to a story from the time of the patriarchs in Genesis 35:16–20. Both Jeremiah and Genesis help illuminate the story that Matthew is telling of the violence at the hand of Herod. The Genesis story records the difficult pregnancy of Rachel in which, just before she dies, she names the child with the pessimistic name Ben-oni, "Son of my sorrow." However, the child's name is changed to Benjamin, "Son of the right hand." The passage in Jeremiah, when read in the context of all of chapter 31, is not one of utter hopelessness, but rather one that speaks of hope and restoration.

The final fulfillment citation is verse 23: "He will be called a Nazorean." The location of this citation from the Hebrew Scriptures is more problematic, because no prophet directly uses these words. Some have suggested parallels to Judges 13:5 and 16:17, which detail the Nazirite vows. It seems most likely, however, that Matthew in wanting to maintain his parallelism, and knowing of Jesus' Nazareth origins, has stretched his sources.

One of the principles of interpretation should always be to interpret any particular text-segment within the context of the whole text. The Matthean birth narrative has connections within the larger text of the gospel. Certain key words foreshadow events that will happen at end of Matthew's gospel. In verses 13 and 19 Matthew references an "angel of the Lord." An angel of the Lord also appears at Jesus' empty tomb (28:1–10) as the one who rolled back the stone. While the parents of Jesus are told to rise in 2:13 and 2:20, in 28:6 the same Greek verb is used to indicate that Jesus has risen from the dead (*egeiro*). Just as Jesus journeys from Egypt to Galilee in 2:19–23, after he has risen he journeys from Jerusalem to Galilee: "Go quickly and tell his disciples, 'He has been raised from the dead, and indeed he is going ahead of you to Galilee'" (28:7). For those knowing the full story, the birth narrative foreshadows the death of Jesus. While Jesus has escaped this initial encounter with the power of the state, the reader is made aware that a death sentence hangs over this infant. The birth narrative of 2:13–23 and the resurrection narrative of 28:1–10 serve as bookends, an *inclusio,* for the words and deeds of Jesus found in between.

In being a sensitive reader for how the evangelist composed this narrative, one quickly notes the portrayal of both Mary and Joseph. Authors typically reveal characters and their traits either by their actions and/or by their words. From the beginning of the birth narrative in 1:18, until the conclusion in 2:13–23, neither Joseph nor Mary say a word. If a Christmas play were based on the birth narrative from Matthew, it would need to be in pantomime. Readers learn about Mary's and Joseph's traits mainly through their actions and by what Matthew explicitly tells. It is up to the reader to see if the actions and the author's descriptions coincide.

A sensitive reader notes the paucity of description about Mary. Unlike the Mary in Luke's birth narrative (Lk. 1:26–56), Mary plays a very quiet role in Matthew's description of Jesus' birth. While Joseph also plays an unassuming role, Matthew reveals more about him. He is a righteous man (1:19), and he is a "son of David" (1:20). What both Mary and Joseph have in common is their depiction as individuals who without hesitation follow God's will. They are being swept along in events of salvation history that are much larger than the immediacy of their experiences.

What the Text-segment Meant to the Community

If verses 13–23 represent a chiasm, a common thread that runs through each section is the ruler Herod. In looking at the overall context of 2:1–23, Herod is mentioned nine times, and in the particular focal segment of 2:13–23, Herod is named five times. By the repetitive use of Herod's name, Matthew makes the heinous ruler's shadow loom large for the interpreters of this particular passage.

This Herod is also known as Herod the Great, who ruled the land of Judea from 37–4 B.C.E. The historical depictions of Herod certainly help set the context for interpreting this passage, especially since Herod and his rule will be set in contrast to the rule of Jesus. Much of the information about Herod can be gleaned from the work of Flavius Josephus, a first-century Judean historian (37–110/120? C.E.). Herod had a privileged background. Sent by his father Antipater to Rome, he was educated and brought up with the elites of Roman society. From the beginning, he was cultivated to be a ruler. When he eventually returned to Israel, he was given military power by his governor father with orders to crush the numerous bandits that operated in the area of Galilee. Through numerous military experiences in these early years Herod became known as a warrior. Eventually, through official Roman sanction, Herod became "king" of Judea. Yet he was always client to his patron Rome.

Herod's concern to maintain his position and honor are well known from the literary records of Josephus and also from what is known in general about how kings protected their honor. Herod was ruthless in dispatching any pretenders to the throne, even his own sons. Caesar Augustus, knowing of the Judean feelings regarding pork and also about Herod's cruelty, once quipped that he would rather be Herod's pig than Herod's son. While no historical records mention Herod's slaughter of the innocents, the episode is certainly within his character. Perhaps the lack of information regarding this slaughter is because for historians of that period this episode in Bethlehem was a rather obscure event not even meriting a footnote in the life of Herod, but it certainly was an important event in the lives of those bereaved of children.

This possibility of the original obscurity of the event is important in considering an assumption that too often writers and preachers make regarding the scale of Herod's slaughter. It is often put forward that hundreds of babies (even thousands) were killed in Bethlehem and the surrounding vicinity. However, Bethlehem was a very small village with, at the most, only a few hundred people. A few infants at the most would have died, not hundreds as is often portrayed. However, the pain of the loss of even a few children in the village was no less than if it were a major city and the deaths were in the hundreds or thousands. One needs to remember that the villages of Judea were tightly knit communities of interlocking kinship groups. Just as it takes a village to raise a child, so does the death of even one infant touch everyone in a village.

This slaughter of the innocents raises a hard question for sensitive readers who struggle with injustices—the question of theodicy. Why does God spare one child but abandon the others to their doom at the bloodstained hands of Herod's henchmen? Or, as one author succinctly puts it, "How could a truly good God permit the Innocents to suffer because of the birth of his Son, whom he hustles off to safety, leaving the others to die? Could he not have spared them all? It is notable that apparently none of the fathers of the others babies in Bethlehem had a night visit from the angel of the Lord."[3] Theodicy questions do not have answers; but they raise our sensitivity to the fact that while hope may be a melody within this story, a corresponding melody of dissonance and pain cannot be ignored.

Interpretive Summary

Matthew presents a stark contrast between two different dynasties. Two different ways of kingship exist: the Herodian, steeped in blood and violence; and the Davidic, grounded in the covenant faithfulness of God. The Herodian dynasty continues with Herod's sons, under whom Rome divided up Palestine into four "governorships." One of these sons is the Archelaus mentioned in the Scripture as taking over after his father's death (2:22). He ruled from 4 B.C.E. to 6 C.E. and continued his father's patterns of abuse and terror. The author of Matthew seems to draw an ironic picture of contrast between two father/son pairs: Herod and Archelaus, and God and Jesus.

In many ways this Matthean story is about inheritance and lineage. The first-century world was one in which lineage conveyed the hope of a future for a family. The Davidic lineage, presented in Matthew 1, is spared; the Herodian lineage is represented in the next generation of Archelaus, and the lineage of the families of Bethlehem is cut off by the death of the sons.

This focus on Herod and his behaviors illustrate one of Matthew's key themes: things are not what they seem.[4] It only *appears* that the Herodian lineage will continue. Herod has disguised his evil intentions with a thin patina of "good intentions." Note for example Herod's words to the wise men that he wants to know where the King of the Judeans is born so that he might also worship. The patina is peeled away with the brutal account of the slaughter of the innocents. Evil will (and does) use any words, means, or disguises, but ultimately, for those who can see, truth will be revealed. It only appears that the Davidic dynasty, represented by Jesus is in exile and fear. Matthew makes this clear with a prayer-statement on the lips of Jesus: "I thank you, Father, Lord of heaven and earth, because you have hidden these things from the wise and the intelligent and have revealed them to infants" (11:25).

Preaching the Passage

The Familiar and Unfamiliar

Most churchgoers, even the occasional ones during the Christmas season, know something of the nativity story—Luke's version, that is, though Matthew's wise men are usually thrown in with the shepherds at the manger scene. Matthew's account is unique. We will need to be careful, therefore, not to harmonize the two accounts. Instead of an infant in a bed of straw, Matthew describes a toddler pursued by a tyrant. Equally unfamiliar are the accounts from the Hebrew Scriptures, a series of four complicated references. The evangelist alludes to: (1) Hosea's reference to the exodus (Hos. 11:1), although likely written during the eighth century B.C.E.; (2) Jeremiah's use of the Rachel story in Genesis (Gen. 35:16–20), although written during the exile; (3) an unknown scriptural reference about Jesus being a "Nazorean"; and (4) possible allusions to the dreams of another Joseph and his encounters with Pharaoh (Gen. 37—50), perhaps a further reference to the exodus. Without question, this is a complex web of scriptural references.

The exodus and the exile—these two Bible stories constitute the heart of what Marcus Borg calls the "macro stories" of the Hebrew Scriptures, stories crucial to the identity of Jews, and, therefore, Jesus.[5] No wonder Matthew is so fond of employing them in this story as a kind of biblical *deja vu*. The tyranny of Egypt's Pharaoh now manifests itself in Rome's Herod. Perhaps by analogy, the preacher will need to explain the significance of these stories for understanding Matthew's gospel in general and this story in particular. Just as it is impossible to understand United States history apart from some familiarity with the Revolutionary War or the Great Depression, hearing Matthew's story demands that our listeners know something of Israel's history (as evidenced by the evangelist's repeated use of Scripture).

Making Connections

Determining how Matthew's two-thousand-year-old story speaks to us today is no easy task, but in this case it is exceptionally complicated. Imagine connecting Rachel's story to Jeremiah's story and Matthew's use of this whole web of stories to twenty-first–century listeners. Such a task seems next to impossible! Just how detailed we wish to be in setting any context, Hebrew Scriptures or otherwise, is a matter of style, although most preachers lean toward one of two extremes: bogging the sermon down in biblical history, or assuming way too much. It helps to recall, in the words of Harry Emerson Fosdick, that folks do not "come to church desperately anxious to discover what happened to the Jebusites,"[6] and that, for some, Gideon is the fellow who went around putting Bibles in all the hotels!

Some may wish to point out the chiastic structure in this text-segment, especially given how often in the past such information has been withheld from congregations. But if we choose to discuss it, how? And in how much detail? Some might opt for a handout or PowerPoint presentation demonstrating the structure in some detail, and how "X marks the spot." Others might offer only a brief analogy: "Everything in this passage points to the middle. There are lots of things to note in Matthew's story, but it is the slaughter of these innocent children that takes center stage."

Another vital part of making connections in sermons relates to identification. Just who are we in this passage for this particular sermon? For Matthew's persecuted church, a comforting reminder of God's protection was just the sort of thing they hoped for. That good news will still preach. You also have the opportunity of calling modern-day disciples to speak out against such social injustice when it raises its head in our time, an all too frequent occurrence.

Thomas Troeger, in a sermon on this passage, attempts to bridge the gap of ancient and modern times by blending them subtly, a somewhat common but effective strategy. After he tells of the angel's warning to Joseph in a dream, Troeger makes clear what is at stake, then and now:

> The human rights policy of Herod's administration is clear:
> > Herod claims all the rights
> > to do with human beings
> > whatever will keep him in power.
>
> A voice shall be heard in Ramah,
> > "wailing and loud lamentation,
> > Rachel weeping for her children."
>
> A voice shall be heard in
> > Poland,
> > > South Africa,
> > > > Central America,
> > > > > Northern Ireland—
> > "wailing and loud lamentation,
> > Rachel weeping for her children."[7]

Patrick J. Willson does something similar, rooting the passage in its historical context, yet blending modern and ancient with alliterated prose:

> Matthew tells us that it is when Herod sits on the throne that the child is born who will be called Emmanuel, God-with-us. Not into any fairy-tale land of "once on a time in a land far away," but into this world of tears and terrorism and tyrants and tragedy, a child is born, and an angel whispers, "Emmanuel, God-with-us."[8]

Innocents Still Slaughtered: Stories for Sermons

Connecting the ancient biblical text and today's congregations is a task made easier with stories. For instance, Jonathan

Kozol shares multiple tales that preachers might use with this text-segment. The first paragraph of his book reads:

> The Number 6 train from Manhattan to the South Bronx makes nine stops in the 18-minute ride between East 59th Street and Brook Avenue. When you enter the train, you are in the seventh richest congressional district in the nation. When you leave, you are in the poorest.[9]

Kozol then shares story after gut-wrenching story about the lives of children in the South Bronx, like the one about a seven-year-old boy named Cliffie who, on a walk with Kozol, is one minute admiring some stuffed bears and the next blurts out, "I shot a boy in the head right over there." Nonchalantly, Cliffie adds, "Would you like a chocolate chip cookie?"[10]

A children's book entitled *The Peaceable Kingdom* is based on Edward Hicks's famous painting by the same name. The inspiration comes in part from the Isaiah passage that envisions a day when lions eat straw, wolves play with sheep, and children are safe even among beasts (Isa. 11:1–9). The preacher might briefly retell the story:

> In the book it seems that the lion, wolf, and leopard manage to get out of Hicks's painting in the museum and find their way into Brooklyn's Botanical Garden. Immediately, the police and fire departments are summoned. Guns are pulled, fire hoses are aimed. Something has to be done about these ferocious beasts. Only these three creatures are not ferocious at all but cowering with fear in a world of guns and violence. Then some children intervene ("and a child shall lead them"). They recognize the animals as belonging to Hicks's painting. In the end the animals are returned to the piece hanging on the wall. And the lion says, "This is more like it. This feels like home." Then he adds, "We had hoped by now that the world would have become a peaceable kingdom."[11]

Of course, the stories used would not need to be limited to children. Not all of "Rachel's children" are infants.

Matthew's Christmas Pageant: A Metaphor

As for the specifics of preparing a sermon, various images and metaphors within the text-segment itself frequently offer us preachers ideas worth considering. Whereas Matthew's three-fold division might have suggested a three-point sermon to previous generations, it is helpful to note that Matthew tells a story here. Today's preacher would do well to do the same! Much has been written in the past twenty-plus years on narrative preaching, including the power of storytelling—biblical and otherwise.[12] A creative blending of Matthew's account, the pertinent allusions to the Hebrew Scriptures, as well as modern stories could help people experience the power of Matthew's story anew. Exposition and experiencing the text are both crucial aspects of preaching!

Jon M. Walton retells the biblical story by backing up into the immediate context:

> The kings (of the three kings fame) had gone to Herod to check on his knowledge of where the Jewish messiah would be born. The magi are asking the established king of the Jews where to find the *new* king of the Jews. Matthew understates the case when he says that Herod was troubled and all Jerusalem with him.
>
> Herod waited to hear back from the itinerant magi, but no word came so he called his astrologers and soothsayers and decided on Bethlehem as his target area. He would kill all the male children under two years of age living in that city. It was reminiscent of Pharaoh's order that all the Hebrew male children should be cast into the Nile, the order that issued Moses into the bullrushes.[13]

In addition to a sermon's structure or flow, preachers ought to consider metaphors or images that might give texture to the sermon. In this case, not only do we have a three-fold structure, but something of a theatrical metaphor as well. Eugene Boring notes how God functions as "the hidden actor"[14] in this drama, behind the scenes (sending magi, warnings in dreams, messages from angels, and so forth). Given the popularity and familiarity of Christmas pageants, maybe the preacher could creatively play with the image of Matthew's Christmas pageant, not with shepherds and the like (as found in Luke's version), but this gospel's account of two very different kings, legitimate (the Christ) and illegitimate (Herod). Thomas Long tells about the annual nativity display at New York's Metropolitan Museum of Art, with all of the usual scenery except for one unique feature: the manger scene is set among ruined Roman columns.[15]

To highlight this tension between the powers, we might begin by playfully juxtaposing Luke's drama with that of Matthew's, only to reveal the horror as the juxtaposition develops. Fred Craddock does something of that in his sermon, "The Hard Side of Epiphany":

> All of our decorations are Luke. They're all from Luke. Madonnas that we've picked up here and there in travel—of wood, one is made of corn, of brass, one made of glass. They're wrapped in tissue and put back in a box like you'd put away crystal or china because they're fragile. Our nativity scene is really cheap, but the kids made it years ago; and we put it out, and it gets prettier every year. But it's from Luke... Luke is over now, and we go to Matthew. Exit the women; in come the men. Exit the stable; now it's a king's palace. Exit the shepherds; in the wise men from the East. Exit the angels, and in comes Herod. We have a little music box. It plays carols—"Silent Night, Holy Night" and "O Little Town of Bethlehem." Just open the lid, and it starts playing. It's on the coffee table. It's Lukan. Music is from Luke. Put the lid down on that, because exit Mary; enter Rachel. Exit lullaby; enter the scream.

"I heard a voice in Ramah. It was Rachel weeping for her children."[16]

Sermon Possibilities

Having explored this text-segment, here are several sermon possibilities:

- The Birth (Death, and Resurrection) of the Christ
- The Protection of God and the Suffering of the Innocents
- Different Kinds of Kingdoms (Peaceful Reign of God)

A Sermon Sampler

The best preaching is never done in isolation. Sometimes we need to get ideas from how others have preached a certain passage. The following four sermons might prove helpful, if only to spark some creative juices in us:

Fred B. Craddock, "The Hard Side of Epiphany," *Wineskins* 2 (1994): 13. The sermon is also available on audiotape as part of the *Preaching Today* series (1986), available through www.preachingtoday.com.

Thomas H. Troeger, untitled sermon in his *Imagining a Sermon* (Nashville: Abingdon Press, 1990), 61–65.

Jon M. Walton, "In the Days of Herod the King," *Pulpit Digest* (November/December 1993): 38.

Patrick J. Willson, "The Massacre of Innocence," *Pulpit Digest* (January/February 1999): 71.

CHAPTER 2

Matthew 4:1–11

Jesus Tempted in the Wilderness

Locating the Sermon

First Sunday of Lent (Year A)

As ministers, we know full well what Lent means. The somberness of Ash Wednesday services is still fresh in our memory, and forty days of serious reflection lie ahead, but not for all churchgoers and certainly not for most folks in the culture around us. Although every Wal-Mart and Target store in the country promotes St. Valentine's Day (with little emphasis on the "saint" part), a line of cards marketing Ash Wednesday (or Lent) has never caught on and probably never will.

In addition, even though we are familiar with the rhythms of the Christian year, Matthew's story of Jesus' temptations in 4:1–11 comes after we have already preached from latter passages in the gospel that show up in Epiphany, including a large portion of the Sermon on the Mount. Most notably, on the Sunday previous to this one (Transfiguration Sunday) the passage is from Matthew 17. Now, one week later, we are back in Matthew 4. To complicate things further, the baptism story in chapter 3, which is the immediate context for the temptation story, was read (and perhaps preached on) weeks ago. Still, there may be some connections on which to draw. So let us begin by examining Matthew 4:1–11.

Understanding the Passage

We often refer to the event in Matthew 4:1–11 (parallels, Mk. 1:12–13 and Lk. 4:1–13) as the "Temptation of Jesus." It is interesting that we use the noun "temptation" to describe this episode in Jesus' life, since nowhere in any of the three gospels do the writers use the noun form. For Mark (1:13) and Luke (4:2) the tempting/testing is a participle form (*peirazomenos*). In the gospel of our interest, Matthew, the form is a passive infinitive (to be tested/tempted, *peirasthenai*, 4:1). By such a subtle shift in labeling this event, interpreters/preachers may miss the focus on the action within this event. This agonistic episode is one in which a reader witnesses intense challenges and responses.[1] If we have domesticated the story into a wonderful tidy and easy triumph for Jesus as he illustrates his messiahship, certainly the gospel writers have not. The ultimate significance of Sonship, and the obedience it entails, hangs in the balance. Readers are left waiting with anticipation to find out which way the balance will tip.

How the Evangelist Crafted the Text-segment

The immediate context of Matthew 4:1–11 conditions to a great extent the way in which an interpreter approaches this episode. The testing of Jesus is located immediately after the baptism of Jesus (3:13–17) and directly before Jesus' public ministry (4:12–17). This traditional order is so well established that it appears in both Mark and Luke as well (with the exception of the inclusion of a genealogy between the baptism and temptation in Lk. 3:23–38). The reason for this sequencing seems clearly based on compositional and theological perspectives. In the previous baptismal scene, Jesus was affirmed by the voice from heaven that he, Jesus, is God's Son and that God is well pleased (3:17). While the voice affirms Jesus, the verisimilitude of this statement still needs confirmation for the listeners/readers. The testings are the vehicles by which the truthfulness of the heavenly claim is confirmed or disproven. As typical in Mediterranean societies, confirmations regarding truth claims must occur in a public venue. Here is a point of irony in Matthew's temptation account. While this account on the surface appears as a private experience occurring only between Jesus and the tempter, it is actually a dramatic episode being observed by the readers. The original listeners will hear this story and give the confirmative evaluation of whether the designation given to Jesus by the heavenly voice is true or not. Of course, based on the evidence presented in the story, the listeners' evaluations confirm the baptismal affirmation that Jesus truly is the honorable Son of God. Two types of honor are integrated in this testing episode. The ascribed honor comes via kinship, i.e., Son of God, and acquired honor comes from achieving honor, via the testing.[2]

Lest any readers/listeners think this scene in 4:1–11 is the first "temptation" of Jesus in Matthew, however, the baptismal scene also illustrates the testing of Jesus. The testing here, however, comes in a different form and from a different source, perhaps even the most unexpected source. A phrase occurs in the concluding verse (v. 11) which, while obscured in English translations, is a clue connecting the baptizing with the testing in the wilderness. In 4:11, after Jesus gives his final riposte to the devil, Matthew writes that the devil "*tote aphiesin auton*" ("then [the devil] let him be"). This same Greek phrase is found in 3:15 after John attempted to prevent Jesus from being baptized: John "*tote aphiesin auton*" (then [he, John] let him be). Jesus, just as he confronted and exorcized the devil in the wilderness, also exorcized his cousin's challenge, which attempted to get Jesus to take a different route of messiahship and Sonship.

The testings of Jesus in the water and the wilderness are not unique but represent the ongoing testing of the Matthean Jesus, which is also found also in the Gethsemane scene (26:36–46). This testing probably climaxes with the challenge to Jesus as he is hanging on the cross, "If you are the Son of God, come down from the cross" (27:40b). The same phrase about Sonship is used by the tempter in the first (4:3) and second challenges (4:6) to Jesus.

One final contextual note regards the text immediately after the testing, that is, Jesus' public ministry (4:12–17). The public ministry of Jesus is set in sharp contrast to the testing episode. If Jesus' private testing takes places in the vague spacial location of the wilderness, Jesus' public ministry is placed within specific geographical locations: Galilee, Nazareth, and Capernaum in the territory of Zebulun and Naphtali. If Jesus is the one being tested/challenged in the wilderness, it is the people who are tested and challenged by Jesus' proclamation: "Repent, for the kingdom of heaven is at hand" (4:17 NAS95). The question is how will the people respond? Will they be honorable sons and daughters of God?

Some explicit and implicit rhetorical and literary patterns are found within the three challenges put to Jesus in this testing. As with 2:13–23, looking at the text-segment's construction may help.

1Then Jesus was led up by the Spirit into the wilderness to be tempted by the devil. 2 He fasted forty days and forty nights, and afterwards he was famished.

> 3 The tempter came and said to him,
>> "If you are the Son of God, command these stones to become loaves of bread."
>>> 4 But he answered, *"It is written,*
>>> † **'One does not live by bread alone,**
>>> **but by every word that comes**
>>> **from the mouth of God.'"**
> 5 Then the devil took him to the holy city and placed him on the pinnacle of the temple,
> 6 saying to him,
>> "If you are the Son of God, throw yourself down; for it is written,

'He will command his angels concerning you,'
and 'On their hands they will bear you up,
so that you will not dash your foot against a stone,'"
      7 Jesus said to him, *"Again it is written,*

> **'Do not put the Lord your God to
> the test.'"**

8 Again, the devil took him to a very high mountain
and showed him all the kingdoms of the world and their
splendor; 9 and he said to him,

> "All these I will give you, if you fall down and
> worship me."

> > 10 Jesus said to him, "Away with you, Satan!
> > *for it is written,*

> > > **'Worship the Lord your God, and
> > > serve only him.'"**

11 Then the devil left him, and suddenly angels came and
waited on him.

The first two tempting-challenges both begin with the
clause, "if you are the Son of God." An interpreter should not
read this initial clause as if the tempter was attempting to place
a doubt in Jesus' mind about his identity. This type of Greek
construction, a third-class conditional sentence, allows for the
translation, *"since* you are the Son of God." Matthew portrays
the tempter as having no doubt about the identity of Jesus.
The question is not identity, but what type of Son of God Jesus
would be. How will this Son of God behave? Will he reflect the
Father?

What perhaps catches the observant reader or listener by
surprise is that in the third challenge (4:9) one expects the same
introductory phrase "if (since) you are the Son" as found in the
previous two (4:3, 6); yet here it is missing. The tempter simply
launches directly into the testing related to all the kingdoms and
glory of the world. A key interpretative principle is that a change
in patterns should always alert a reader to pay close attention.

J. Ramsey Michaels suggests that the first two testings are aimed at Jesus' divinity and specifically as a challenge to Jesus' divine Sonship.[3] The third testing-challenge, however, is directed to Jesus' humanity: "It is as if the tempter has taken to heart the two previous responses of Jesus as man, and deliberately chosen to approach him on human terms... The third is unmistakably aimed at his humanity, and at the greed and ambition that characterize human nature."[4] This testing, perhaps, is recalled later in Matthew when Jesus instructs his disciples via the rhetorical question: "For what will it profit them if they gain the whole world but forfeit their life?" (Mt. 16:26a).

Another discernible pattern within 4:1–11 is Jesus' repetitive use of the Hebrew Scriptures (vv. 4, 7, 10) in his riposte to the testing-challenges issued by the tempter. The responses from Scripture are specifically from Deuteronomy and are examined below.

The author of Matthew in this testing episode brings together several different allusions from the Hebrew Scriptures tradition, no doubt an indication of his sensitivity to an audience that is steeped in the traditional stories and images of the Hebrew Scriptures. The setting in the wilderness, the forty days, the three scriptural references from Deuteronomy, and food miraculously provided by God all call attention to the exodus experience. The exodus experience was not a distant and disconnected experience for the people who originally heard this narrative. It continued to function as one of their central "macro stories" by which they ordered their identity.[5] To hear this story reinforced the belief in the God who sustains and is dependable.

Along with the exodus motifs we also hear echoes of exile. The exile serves as another meta-narrative that provided identity and meaning for the Judean people. Some within Judean society understood the wilderness/exile as still being experienced— ironically and painfully, within their own land! The occupation by the Romans was a constant and incarnate reminder of their present wilderness. If the people of God were still experiencing the wilderness of exile, then they needed one who could lead them out, one who would not only proclaim that the exile was over but whose actions could demonstrate it.[6] Jesus' victory in the wilderness, at the very beginning of his ministry, was an assurance that the exile was coming to an end and that a new leader, like Moses but greater, had arrived.

Jesus' victory in the testing-challenge also provides a window on the true source of the struggles and conflict the Judeans experienced. In the previous narratives, Jesus and his family were under threat from Herod and his son Archelaus (2:1–23), representatives of the Roman/Judean authorities. This conflict between two earthly kingdoms, however, was only the facade of the true battle being waged. This testing narrative demonstrated in a highly dramatic fashion that, to use Pauline terms, the contest is not "against enemies of blood and flesh, but against the rulers, against the authorities, against the cosmic powers of this present darkness, against the spiritual forces of evil in the heavenly places" (Eph. 6:12). For the author of Matthew, the Roman Empire is only a facade behind which the Devil lurks. It is the Devil who controls kingdoms and the earthly rulers who are his client-puppets (4:9). At least in this one story, the curtain is stripped away, and the devilish puppet master is revealed. The question is, Will the tempter be able to pull the strings to make the Son of God behave like the sons of the empire?

This revealing behind the scene struggle echoes the message in Revelation. John in Revelation portrays the true power behind the beast of the Roman Empire to be the "great dragon..., that ancient serpent, who is called the Devil and Satan, the deceiver of the whole world" (Rev. 12:9a). Just as the misplaced worship of the beast is a focus in Revelation, the climatic testing for Jesus is also about worship. This final testing is for Jesus to misdirect his worship from God to the devil (4:9). Jesus passes the testing and is not deceived as to the true nature of evil or its desire to manipulate. Just as Jesus is given the title of "faithful witness" in Revelation 1:5, so also in the testing narrative he demonstrates by words and actions his faithfulness.

What the Text-segment Meant to the Community

As noted above, the Greek word for testing in Matthew 4:1 is a passive infinitive (*peirasthenai*). When passive constructions are used in the New Testament, they often signal that God is the one who is ultimately in control and guiding what is taking place, i.e., the grammatical/theological label of "divine passive." The author of Matthew wants to make clear two important points. First, God is the ultimate and total sovereign even though the tempter boasts about controlling and distributing the kingdoms of the world. Second, and perhaps most important, God reflects the typical Mediterranean behavior of a father who tests his son. The parenting experience in the traditional Mediterranean culture has little in common with contemporary parenting practices.[7] Sons were strictly disciplined, even to the point of extreme physical punishment. The writer of Sirach presents these words of parenting wisdom:

> He who loves his son will whip him often, so that he may rejoice at the way he turns out... Bow down his neck in his youth, and beat his sides while he is young, or else he will become stubborn and disobey you and you will have sorrow of soul from him. Discipline your son and make his yoke heavy, so that you may not be offended by his shamelessness. (Sir. 30:1, 12–13)

This strict discipline/testing sought to assure that sons would demonstrate submissive authority to the father and loyalty to the family. The question always dominating a traditional society was whether the son would honor or shame the father and family. Jesus is tested by his father. In this episode Jesus' testing bears resemblance to the testing of Isaac by Abraham (Gen. 22). Isaac is the faithful son who never flinches from what appears inevitable. Jesus, likewise, chooses to honor his father and prove himself the faithful Son.

In this narrative, Jesus "exorcizes" the devil in a very specific way. Note the command to the devil in verse 10: "Away with you,

Satan." This language is reminiscent of exorcism terminology. Typically in ancient exorcisms, one used amulets, manual gestures with the hand, or incantations to ward off evil spirits. Jesus the exorcist resorts to none of these typical exorcism tools in his encounter with the devil; rather Jesus defeats the devil via Scripture. Scripture was the resource available, at least in oral form, to every listener or reader of this narrative. Whatever a Judean might encounter in daily life, Scripture was available to bring help.

The specific Scriptures Jesus quoted originate within the context of Deuteronomy. In the first instance, Jesus is responding to the testing-challenge of hunger. He recites a portion of Deuteronomy 8:3. As is always important when the Hebrew Scriptures are cited, a preacher/interpreter should return to the original context of the citation. The context of Deut. 8:1–20 is a call to remember how the Lord provided in the midst of the exodus experience.

In the second testing scene, the voice of Scripture comes from an unusual source. The tempter cites Psalm 91:11a, 12. This use of Scripture, however, is a shallow parody of Jesus' usage. As one writer states, "The devil has misused the scripture by confusing trust in God with a presumption that makes God a servant of human bidding."[8] Jesus, on the other hand, recites a part of Deuteronomy 6:16, again a story from the exodus. It reinforces the view that one should not doubt (test) the faithfulness of God, who is able to provide.

For the third testing-challenge, the quote comes from Deuteronomy 6:13. In considering this quote from the Hebrew Scripture, one might note that Jesus' citation is not verbatim. Jesus replaces "fear" with worship, since this seems to be a critical focus in Matthew; and Jesus adds "only" to illustrate that loyalty is due to God alone.

Only in a comparison between the Matthean and Lukan testing accounts does one discern the importance of this last climatic temptation. The order of the second and third temptations are reversed in Matthew and Luke. The pivotal testing-challenge in Matthew is bowing to and worshiping the tempter, while in Luke it is jumping off the pinnacle of the temple. Matthew orients his gospel toward the importance of worship that focuses on God and not on displaced idolatrous objects or persons. Those in Matthew who are most commended or shown as righteous correctly understand the proper focus of worship. What is ironic is that frequently worship in Matthew is directed not to God, but to Jesus. The gospel ends with the disciples specifically worshiping the resurrected Jesus (28:9, 17). For Matthew, to worship Jesus is to worship God.

Interpretive Summary

For readers, the "Testing of Jesus" primarily reveals the identity of Jesus. It not only illustrates that Jesus is the Son of God, but it also presents the type of Son he will be. He is a Son who is honorable and worthy. Some of the secondary emphases revolve around the providence of God, the good news that the exile of the present age is coming to an end, and that everyone has access to the resource of Scripture during times of testing.

Preaching the Passage

The Shape of Matthew's Story

Most every commentary notes the close relation of the baptism story with the temptation story, but last week's transfiguration story (for those who preach the Lectionary) may be of more help than we first realize. Both the transfiguration and temptation narratives are mountain stories, an important part of Matthew's crafting of his gospel, which may help with our own crafting of the sermon.

Preachers intrigued by this emphasis on mountains may choose to point this out in the sermon—remembering, of course, that not all listeners will be so fascinated. The preacher might say:

In Matthew's gospel so much of the big stuff happens on mountains, suspended between heaven and earth. Six such mountain stories appear in this gospel. Last week we considered the one about Transfiguration. It happened on a mountain! Now we look at Matthew's first mountain story, the temptation of Jesus. It begins in the desert and reaches its climax on a mountain.

Others might consider the emphasis on mountains in the study but not overtly refer to it in the sermon. This is yet another of the many decisions we must make every week. Not every thought while seated at our desks needs be repeated in the pulpit. That even includes some of our best thoughts from time to time. There will be other Sundays, other sermons.

Whether we highlight the emphasis on mountains or not, this type of story is one we shall encounter over and over in Matthew's gospel. *Pronouncement stories,* or, more simply, *stories about* Jesus, are obviously abundant in the gospels. As the latter term implies, these kinds of passages tell us something about the unique identity of Jesus (in this case, his refusal to conform to the ways of the tempter), but they do more than just that. These stories imply a subtle message for how *disciples* are expected to live as well, both then and now.[9]

Making Connections

As for helping listeners to make sense of stories about Jesus, an analogy might be just the ticket. Sometimes the only way we can understand a new idea is by comparing it with a familiar one.[10] It is hard to imagine listeners unfamiliar with pronouncement stories of some kind, no matter their cultural background. In the United States, we need only recall Rosa Parks's bus ride, a story with social ramifications that have reverberated down through the years. A simple reference like that can help listeners understand the two aspects of first-century pronouncement stories—remembrance and repentance.

As we have seen before (Mt. 2:13–23), the web of story connections in Matthew's gospel is often complex. In this case, Matthew's story of Jesus tempted for forty days in the wilderness echoes back to Israel's own temptations for forty years in the wilderness, one of the key differences being the faithfulness of Jesus versus Israel's failings. While the Revised Common Lectionary chooses to use readings from the Genesis narratives (2:15–17; 3:1–7), some preachers might choose one of the many wilderness passages in the Hebrew Scriptures to which Matthew refers.

Chapter breaks in Scripture are necessary, but often unfortunate. If the preacher considers the parallels with the baptism and temptation stories crucial enough to mention in the sermon, then perhaps the Scripture reading on this Sunday could span from 3:13 to 4:11 without interruption. Sometimes it helps to remember there is no such thing as the "Lectionary Police," at least not officially sworn-in officers.

In some traditions it is common that those seeking baptism on Easter use the season of Lent as a time of preparation. If so, this would be an excellent opportunity to note this before the whole congregation. As an extension of Matthew's church, we learn from this passage about our Lord's obedience and countercultural resistance. We, too, as baptized children of God, are called to live differently.

Once again the passage is a story. Such a simple insight could go unnoticed. We who weekly look for material to put in our sermons, often neglect one of the most obvious items—the text-segment itself. A retelling of this story, along with an impassioned reading of the passage, can be one of the high points of the worship experience. Or, as we have considered before (Mt. 2:13–23), we might weave an ancient retelling with modern details, such as William Willimon does:

> If you are the Son of God, Jesus, turn these stones into bread, give us a sense of inner peace, help us make it through the week, keep my children chaste and pure, fix

my marriage, help me with my financial problems—and then we shall worship you.[11]

In a similar fashion, Charles Campbell paraphrases the second temptation:

Take charge of the biological weapons, deploy some troops, command the implementation of a "Star Wars" missile defense system. All the kingdoms can be yours—if you will just use the world's means of power: domination and violence.[12]

Since none of us can relate to the specifics of these three temptations contemporary analogies such as Campbell's are useful.

The Empire Strikes Back: Stories for Sermons

For most listeners, the empire striking back evokes scenes from the *Stars Wars* movies, which may or may not prove helpful in our sermons. For us, however, such an image should also evoke scholarly understanding of this ancient passage. Warren Carter's emphasis is most beneficial here. He notes that if the tempter is in a position to offer "all the kingdom/empires of the world," then this "startling revelation means that Satan controls the Roman empire."[13]

We may choose, then, to preach on this passage in light of international political practices. Nelson Mandela's account of the Apartheid practices in South Africa is a powerful testimony of the empire's dominion in recent times.[14]

If we choose to tell stories of modern-day temptations closer to home—ours personally or those of our listeners in general—we will need to avoid trivializing the text-segment. This is not about having dessert with our meal, even if we did give it up for Lent. The scope and gravity of the text demands a larger scale, a grander view of the world. A passage's mood is not something to be ignored, especially given the surreal aspects of this text-segment.[15]

Another way to help listeners relate to an ancient text-segment is to acknowledge openly the distance they might be experiencing. Paul Scherer, the great Presbyterian preacher, began a sermon on this passage by referring to it as Matthew's "weird story." He acknowledges what many listeners must have been feeling about a showdown between Jesus and the devil:

> No doubt it seemed almost unintelligibly remote when it was read to you—those two shadowy figures weaving in and out like gigantic silhouettes against the dawn. What on earth could it have to do with us? That there should be anything contemporaneous about it is a notion which scarcely ever occurs to anybody.[16]

The use of contemporary stories can also prove helpful, as Thomas Long has done in a sermon in which he begins with three contemporary vignettes. In one of them he tells of dealing with a rude salesperson in a hardware store. Long says, "I was tempted to go back up there and give him a piece of my mind! I was *tempted*...what does that mean?" These lighthearted stories allow listeners to ease into the sermon, and only then does Long move to the heart of the matter, noting how common understandings of temptation miss the mark:

> In ordinary terms, we think of temptation as the urge to do something we really would like to do but know we shouldn't do—one more cigarette, one more fling, one more drink, one more juicy rumor. But the deepest temptation is not the urge to misbehave, to do what we know we shouldn't do, but rather the enticement to compromise our baptismal identity, to be who we are not called to be.[17]

Fred Craddock, in his sermon "Tempted to Do Good," begins innocently enough, too, before inviting listeners to wade into the "deeper end of the pool and listen to this text." When he finally does, the mood of the sermon gets serious:

Temptation at its deepest level has nothing to do with key lime pie or chocolate fudge. It has nothing to do with that piece of paper in the pocket that has the answers to the test. It has nothing to do with a half pint in the tool chest. Jesus' temptation was this: What am I going to do with my life?... So Jesus, what are you going to do with the rest of your life? Still wet from his baptism, now he faces it.[18]

William Willimon, formerly dean of students at Duke University, compares Jesus' beginning of ministry with that of college graduates deciding what to do with their lives. Will the baptized live up to that calling?[19] Perhaps this is a helpful image for all our listeners, many of whom in today's society are constantly rethinking their life goals.

Stephen King offers a fascinating short story entitled "The Man in the Black Suit." This modern story offers some interesting contrasts and comparisons for today's preacher. A summary will not do it justice, and besides, most of us need to include some popular literature on our reading lists. The collection in which it appears is full of short stories that preachers might find interesting.[20]

Perhaps the best-known piece of literature that deals with temptation is Dostoevsky's treatment of this very passage from Matthew in his classic novel, *The Brothers Karamazov*. Ivan reads aloud to his brother a story he has been working on in which the Christ comes back to earth during the Spanish Inquisition. Again comes the conflict Jesus encountered in the first century, only instead of the religious authorities going to the civil leaders (as recorded in the gospels), the Cardinal himself has Jesus arrested. The Cardinal of Seville claims at length that what the "dread spirit" offered in the wilderness impacted "the whole future history of the world and of mankind," and that Jesus chose wrongly. The old Cardinal gloats:

We accepted from him what You had rejected with indignation, the last gift he offered You—all the kingdoms of earth. We accepted Rome and Caesar's sword from *him,* and we proclaimed ourselves the sole rulers of the earth... But You, You could have taken Caesar's sword when You came the first time. Why did You reject that last gift?... Had You accepted Caesar's purple, You would have founded a universal empire... So we took Caesar's sword and, by taking it, we rejected You and followed *him.*[21]

The movie *The Mission* tells the story of the church's temptation to do things the world's way instead of keeping the vows of baptism. It's based on the real-life accounts of missionaries in South America during the 1750s. But while missionaries have come bringing the good news of the gospel, mercenaries have come to make slaves. The movie contrasts two ways of being in the world: the way of the cross as seen in the life of Father Gabriel versus the way of the sword as evidenced in Captain Mendoza.

In a surprising twist of events, Mendoza is converted to Christianity. As penance, he carries his old armor up the mountain, to where the Indians he once persecuted live. In one of the film's most powerful scenes, Mendoza undergoes a baptism of sorts, immersed through a waterfall and forgiven. The challenge for him, as for all of God's baptized children, is to live up to his vows—to renounce his old ways. When the decision is made to close down the mission, the two ways become even more evident. Mendoza goes back to fighting, even if it is for the ways of Christ, while Father Gabriel remains true to his vows. While Mendoza sharpens his old rusty sword, Father Gabriel prepares for worship. Nowadays, some might choose to show an actual clip from the movie, but even if not, a retelling could be a powerful moment of the sermon event.

Sermon Possibilities

As is always the case with scriptures, there are multiple options for preachers to ponder:

• Christ's Faithfulness in Light of Israel's/Our Failures
• The Empire's Domain

A Sermon Sampler

It is hard to find three better-known contemporary preachers whose sermons are worth studying than Fred Craddock, Thomas Long, and William Willimon. Add to that the voice of Paul Scherer, and most of us will find some ideas for our own sermons.

Fred B. Craddock, "Tempted to Do Good," in *The Cherry Log Sermons* (Louisville: Westminster John Knox Press, 2001), 13–18.

Thomas G. Long, "Facing Up to Temptation," in *Whispering the Lyrics: Sermons for Lent and Easter* (Lima, Ohio: CSS, 1995), 17–24.

Paul Scherer, "Let God Be God," in *The Word God Sent* (Grand Rapids: Baker, 1965), 143–52.

William H. Willimon, "Getting What We Want," in *Pulpit Resource* 27 (1999): 31–34.

CHAPTER 3

Matthew 5:1–12

The Beatitudes of Jesus

Locating the Sermon

Fourth Sunday after Epiphany (Year A)

For those who preach from the Revised Common Lectionary, this week's passage comes on the heels of Jesus calling his first disciples (4:12–23), an account that ends by naming healing as a kind of proclamation. What may be missing, however, with a reading that begins with 5:1 and Jesus' Beatitudes, is the description of the crowds at the end of chapter 4 (4:23–25). "Those who were afflicted with various diseases and pains, demoniacs, epileptics, and paralytics" (4:24) hardly constituted the religious "who's who" of Jesus' day—or our day either, for that matter.

As we shall see, Jesus' words of favor are pronounced on those least likely to be considered worthy in the ancient as well as modern world. Like so much of the wisdom in the gospels, the truth of God is counter to a worldview consumed with success (not purity of heart), fame (not famine), power (not peacemaking), and money (not poverty of spirit). Ironically, in some years this passage falls on the same Sunday as the Super Bowl, a portrait of America's addiction to entertainment and big money. The words of Jesus in this passage envision a different way of being in the world. Before we look, however, at what this passage says to us today, let us once again begin with the ancient text-segment.

Understanding the Passage

Besides the "Ten Commandments" and the "Golden Rule," the Beatitudes in Matthew 5:1–12 are one of the most recognizable passages in either of the Bible's testaments. This familiarity, however, both for the preacher and the person in the pew can breed the deadly attitude of, "Ho hum—I have heard these 'blesseds' all before." For a preacher, however, Matthew 5:1–12 can present an opportunity to open a new window onto the messages in the gospel of Matthew. Verses 1–12 provide clues for understanding the community of Matthew, for understanding Jesus' message about the reign of God, and for challenging contemporary Christians about their identities in a larger society.

How the Evangelist Crafted the Text-segment

The context of Matthew 5:1–12 is formed by the few verses that precede it in 4:23–25. In these verses the author gives a succinct summary of the ministry of Jesus, who has gone about in Galilee "teaching in their synagogues and proclaiming the good news of the kingdom and curing every disease and every sickness among the people" (v. 23). At this point in the gospel, the author has not presented lengthy narratives to demonstrate the content of Jesus' teaching. In this list of Jesus' ministry activities, however, perhaps it is significant that teaching is listed first. All of chapters 5 through 7 illustrate that Jesus is a rabbi who not only competes with the best teachers in the Judean tradition, but who surpasses all the scribes by his words (7:28). These sapient words of Jesus in Matthew 5—7 have been collectively christened the "Sermon on the Mount."

The Sermon on the Mount (Mt. 5—7) functions as the first of five lengthy discourses that the rabbi Jesus will deliver to either crowds and/or disciples. Some textual cues make

it easy to recognize these Matthean discourses as distinct
units of thought. For example, after each discourse the writer
concludes with words such as, "Now when Jesus had finished
saying these things…" (7:28a), or, "When Jesus had finished
saying all these things…" (26:1a).[1] Besides the Sermon on the
Mount, the other discourses include Matthew 10:1–42, teaching
about mission and discipleship; Matthew 13:1–52, teaching in
parables; Matthew 18:1–35, teaching about true greatness and
community integrity; and Matthew 23:1—25:46, a teaching
and warning about Judean leadership. These five teaching
discourses echo the frequent Matthean theme of Jesus as the
new Moses. Just as Moses in the Judean tradition received the
new teachings/laws from God and delivered them to the people
in the form of the Pentateuch, the five books of law, so Jesus
as the one greater than Moses, but firmly within the Judean
tradition, presents the renewed teachings/laws to the people
of God in five discourses.

By standing first in the discourses, the Sermon on the Mount
inaugurates Jesus' authoritative words about the community
and the reign of God. This position makes the Beatitudes of
crucial importance. If, as Dale Allison proposes, the core of
the Sermon on the Mount is constituted by 5:13—7:12, then
Matthew 5:1–12 serves the important literary function as an
introduction for the heart of Jesus' teaching.[2] As in any oral
presentation, one wants to engage the listeners in a positive way
before presenting the core of a teaching or sermon, especially
one with challenging ethical admonitions. What 5:3–12 does is
to present an opening word of encouragement to the listeners.
Before there is any admonishments or words of challenge, Jesus
presents, from his perspective, the kingdom pedigree of his
listeners. He invests them with some under-appreciated and
surprising characteristics, as will be noted below.

Matthew 5:1–12 demonstrates a high level of sophistication
in its composition. It illustrates classic literary and rhetorical
strategies for engaging both reader and listener. For example,
the Beatitudes are divided into three distinct units or stanzas.
The first four Beatitudes in verses 3–6 represent, respectively,

those who are poor in spirit, who mourn, who are meek, and who hunger and thirst for righteousness. The second group of four Beatitudes in verses 7–10 represent those who are merciful, pure in heart, peacemakers, and persecuted for righteousness sake. The ninth, final, and climatic Beatitude in verses 11–12 is directed to those who are persecuted because of their intimate relationship/association with Jesus.

Several examples of the author's literary skill are evident here. Note the clear parallelism and pattern that occur within and between the Beatitudes in the first and second units or stanzas. The first stanza (vv. 3–6) has a series of four Beatitudes following a pattern of A-B, A-B, A-B, A-B. The first part, A, affirms a particular characteristic demonstrated by the listeners, while part B gives the warrant/reward for this affirmation. The second stanza (vv. 7–10) follows the same pattern. This parallelism is also reflected in the how the last Beatitude in each stanza, vv. 6 and 10, focuses on the identical theme of righteousness. The parallelism is also found in the equal length of each stanza and in the use of the third person address.

While verses 3–6 and 7–10 are parallel, they are also connected by the author's use of an *inclusio* or bookend around the Beatitudes found in verses 4–9. The first Beatitude in verse 3, the beginning bookend, indicates that the promise for the poor in spirit is that "theirs *is* the kingdom of heaven." All the rest of the promises in the Beatitudes up to verse 10, however, are not in the present tense but the future tense: "they *will...*" It is only with the eighth Beatitude in verse 10 that the author returns once again to the present tense to indicated that for the persecuted "theirs *is* the kingdom of heaven." With a brilliant stroke of the pen, the author has framed the future experiences that Christians will obtain between the present reality of the kingdom of heaven, which is already theirs. The tension between what is and what will be reflects the reality of Matthew's eschatological perspective of a reign of God that is both future and present.

The ninth and final Beatitude (vv. 11–12) stands in contrast to the previous eight. First, it is the longest of all the Beatitudes with its expanded description of what persecution will entail. What stands out most, however, might be the sudden shift from third person to second person: "Blessed are *you...*" (v. 11). If the original listeners thought that Jesus was directing these Beatitudes at another group besides themselves, they were shocked back into reality by the fact that Jesus had been speaking about them all the time. This last Beatitude, therefore, serves as a warning that they can expect to experience persecution and to have a garbage heap of evil words dumped on their heads. It also, however, provides encouragement; they have the same honor and status as the most famous and respected prophets from the past, such as Isaiah, Jeremiah, Amos, and Hosea. To live out their lives as peacemakers, as the meek, and by embracing the other attributes meant living a prophetic lifestyle that publicly declared that they were participants in the reign of God.

It is always helpful to study the Beatitudes in Matthew's Sermon on the Mount with the parallel Beatitudes from the Sermon on the Plain in Luke 6:20–26. The importance of the comparison is not to harmonize, of course, but to observe what is uniquely Matthean and what is uniquely Lukan. Most easily seen is that Luke presents a much shorter version, citing only four Beatitudes. Luke does include four woes (vv. 24–26) that parallel the four blessings (vv. 20–23). And, while Luke's version has the framing device of the present tense around the future tense like Matthew's, the Beatitudes in Luke are worded differently.

The difference in wording reflects a Lukan theological perspective that is both different from and yet similar to Matthew's. For example, Luke does not "spiritualize" the concept of the poor, but bluntly words his first Beatitude as "Blessed are you who are poor..." (Lk. 6:20). One other obvious difference in this particular Beatitude, which is reflected in all the Lukan Beatitudes, is the use of the second person plural:

"...for yours is the kingdom of God" (Lk. 6:20). While Matthew withholds the surprise identification until the last, Luke from the beginning connects his listener with the characteristics and reward in the Beatitudes.

What the Text-segment Meant to the Community

Because of its constant repetition, the word *blessed* cannot be ignored in the Beatitudes. The term typically translated as "blessed" in English is the Greek word *makarios,* which is translated into Latin as *beatitudo,* from which English gets the title "The Beatitudes." In most modern translations the tradition of translating *makarios* as blessed is very strong. Some translators have attempted to make explicit that it is God who is behind this action, "God blesses..." (*Contemporary English Version, New Living Translation*). Other translators, realizing the difficulty of translating *makarios,* have attempted to find a different term to capture its meaning, such as, "Happy are..." (*Today's English Version, Jerusalem Bible, J. B. Phillips, New Century Version*). The traditional translation of "blessed" and the modern translation of "happy" or "fortunate," however, do not adequately capture the spirit of *makarios,* especially as it is understood in its first-century social and cultural context.

One of the most insightful observations on how to understand the essence of *makarios* comes from K.C. Hanson.[3] The term *makarios* occurs within a specific value system within a particular culture. Specifically, *makarios* occurs within a social and cultural system that is dominated by shame and honor; therefore, a contemporary reader should seek appropriate terms to capture what the original listeners would have heard and understood. Perhaps the best terms to translate *makarios* could be "esteemed" or "honored." Listen to an example (5:3–6) of how the Beatitudes might be heard when using terms such as "honored" and "esteemed."

Honored are the poor in spirit, for theirs is the kingdom of heaven.

Honored are those who mourn, for they will be comforted.
Esteemed are the meek, for they will inherit the earth.
Esteemed are those who hunger and thirst for
righteousness, for they will be filled.

Reading the Beatitudes from this perspective radically alters how one understands them. Honor was not readily available to all people, especially the individuals to whom Jesus addressed his words. Honor was based on accepted status, often status associated with lineage (note the importance of a genealogy at the beginning of Matthew's gospel, 1:1–15). In this radical reordering of a worldview, however, Jesus is investing—or, perhaps better, *endowing*—with honor those who are the most unlikely candidates to have honor. The typical peasant audience to whom Jesus addressed these Beatitudes would never imagine that their status could in any way ever be considered as "honorable." To be hungry, poor, meek, and mournful is to carry the burden of weakness and the inability to maintain one's position—one's honor. In other words, the original audience carried in their lives the cultural and social stigma of shame.

What Jesus offered was a radical reordering of the perceived wisdom about how the world defined who was honorable. For example, in the ancient Mediterranean world of the first century, the honored were those who conquered and displayed might. These were the ones who could and did inherit the earth, i.e., territory. The powerful warriors of old such as Alexander the Great and the heroes of the Judean tradition such as King David, even the client-kings of Rome like Herod the Great, illustrate that territory is taken and held by the strong. To be meek is to be nobody and to have nothing. Jesus' wisdom, however, was that no longer are the mighty honored, but those with little or nothing. Richard Hays captures well this reordered world view: "To be trained for the kingdom is to be trained to see the world from the perspective of God's future—and therefore askew from what the world counts as common sense."[4]

The Beatitudes begin by endowing listeners with honor. Jesus' last discourse in Matthew (23:1—25:46) ends with listeners, specifically the scribes and Pharisees, being castigated for their shameful behavior. In Matthew 23, a recurring theme-word is "woe," in Greek *ouai*. Again Hanson suggests that the social and cultural context of the ancient world should dictate how we translate and understand this closing discourse. Instead of the typical translation "woe," he suggests "how shameful!"[5] The original listeners would have heard Jesus' words in this way: "*Shame on* you scribes and Pharisees, hypocrites! For you tithe mint, dill, and cummin, and have neglected the weightier matters of the law: justice and mercy and faith" (23:23a). Therefore one can read all the teachings and deeds of Jesus in Matthew as being framed by words that endow honor on his peasant followers and with words of reproach for some of the scribes and Pharisees.[6]

Interpretive Summary

While the first eight Beatitudes all deal with ethical behavior, and specifically ethical behavior lived out in the context of community, the last Beatitude is different. As noted above, it shifts from the pattern of third person as found in the previous eight to the second person: "you." Also, and perhaps most importantly, the listener is directed to his or her own relationship with Jesus. Persons have honor bestowed on them because of the persecutions they have experienced on account of Jesus (v. 11).

What is striking in this Beatitude is the absence of any retaliations for the three-fold challenges—reviling, persecuting, and speaking evil against—that fall on a follower of Jesus. A follower is persecuted but does not respond back by way of violence. The last Beatitude foreshadows Jesus' later words in the Sermon on the Mount: "But I say to you, Love your enemies and pray for those who persecute you" (5:44). This emphasis on enduring persecution (for Jesus' sake and in the name of love) was one of the most frequently cited sayings of

Jesus in the second century.[7] After Constantine (who reigned from 306 to 337) sanctioned Christianity as the religion of the empire early in the fourth century, however, no longer were Christians persecuted as the state's enemies. The love command, therefore, became more restricted to "the personal realm or more frequently totally confined to a select group of Christians in religious communities, either in monastic orders or, since the Reformation, to people generally dismissed as 'enthusiasts.'"[8] In this last Beatitude, as in the previous ones, the community of God never sought to found God's reign and will through violence. They lived in active anticipation of what God was doing and would do in their lives as they lived out a community ethic of love in the face of persecution.

Preaching the Passage
The Sermon's Grammar: Vocabulary and Verbs

In this passage not only do we have another mountain story (see Mt. 4:1–11), we have something other than story—Beatitudes. Of course, nobody except church folks use the term, and many regular attendees may not fully understand it. Robert Schuller's popular book *The Be (Happy) Attitudes* certainly has not helped, a self-help approach to the reign of God if ever there were one: "I'm really hurting—but I'm going to bounce back!"[9]

The term *beatitude* is from the Middle English, meaning perfect happiness, as in *beatific* vision. Thus, Jesus announces a vision of "perfect happiness" on his followers. To do so, he employs the word *blessed,* with which each beatitude begins. As already noted, this, too, is a strange word to our ears. Even in a sandwich shop for lunch, someone sneezes and a kind person offers, "God bless you"; but this is not the same word.

Hopefully, our sermons will reflect the same precision of language found in the *original* text-segment. English translations have offered several alternatives to "blessed" ("happy," "congratulations," "honored," "favored"), but whichever one we choose, we will need to bear in mind not only the original meaning versus what we prefer, but what modern words convey today.[10] How will listeners hear the words with which we interpret Jesus' teaching?

It is not just the text-segment's words that we should note, but verb tenses, too. All of the Beatitudes begin in the present tense, "Blessed are..." The initial phrase of each beatitude emphasizes *now,* not the future. The stress, however, is not exclusively present. With the exception of verses 3 and 10, the concluding focus is in the future: "...for they *will...*" As Warren Carter points out, "Beatitudes are directed to the present and future ages,"[11] which is as it should be in the church's preaching. Most likely, we will need to explain what it means to live between Christ's first and second comings. Matters of eschatology (inaugurated or otherwise) can be complicated even for preachers, but our explanations need not be overly elaborate.

Equally important is the mood of the Beatitudes. Jesus speaks primarily in the indicative, how things are; not the imperative, how things should be. As Stanley Hauerwas and William Willimon note, "The Beatitudes are not a strategy for achieving a better society, they are an indication, a picture. A vision of the inbreaking of a new society."[12] First and foremost, therefore, the Beatitudes are indicative portrayals of a different world order. Still, most scholars acknowledge a degree of "implicit command" woven into their fabric as well.[13] Sermons rarely get preached in the indicative mode these days, despite the overwhelming indicative and descriptive nature of the Bible's stories.[14] If we follow Jesus' lead here, perhaps the imperative pulses of the sermon will be more subtle, less hortatory.

For Whose Ears? Two Tiers of Listeners

Since Jesus is not named in the Greek text of Matthew 5:1–12, the pronouns make us include the context. Rightly so. Clearly we are to understand that Jesus' listeners included the social misfits named at the end of the previous chapter (4:23–25), although some have suggested that while the disciples form the main congregation for Jesus' sermon, the crowds as well overhear his teachings.[15] As preachers, therefore, we must think about the people to whom we are preaching. "As in real estate, so also in the interpretation of Scripture," write Stanley Saunders and Charles Campbell, "the most important principles are location, location, location."[16]

Just who are the people to whom we will announce Jesus' words of favor? Beatitudes that pronounce God's favor with the poor sound different in the poorer parts of town than coming from ministers in gowns. Even if we know well the people to whom we preach, they are most certainly at different points in life, positions of privilege, and the like. Shall we preach this coming Sunday as an act of social protest or to bring comfort to God's troubled saints, even if some of their troubles are peculiar to North America's middle class? Preachers familiar with Fred Craddock's notion of "overhearing the gospel" might even try creative possibilities in which the sermon is not directly addressed to the congregation, but relays Jesus' words of blessing, allowing those who "listen in" to make application themselves. That concept, while appealing, is somewhat harder to pull off than traditional styles of proclamation. Therefore, we turn our attention next to the importance of stories in sermons.

Contemporary Experiences of Blessedness: Stories and Images

Thomas Long compares the Sermon on the Mount to the United States Constitution and the Beatitudes to its preamble. "The Beatitudes proclaim what is, in light of the kingdom of heaven, unassailably true. They describe the purpose of every holy law, the foundation of every custom, the aim of every practice of this new society, this colony of the kingdom, the church called and instructed by Jesus."[17] Although such an analogy might be mistaken for endorsing the blending of church and state, the analogy is still a helpful one.

William Willimon offers a wonderful analogy for understanding Jesus' words not as command, but as gift. He tells about a high school teacher he had who bored the class for hours on end with lectures about English history—royalty, dates, battles, that sort of thing. One of students finally asked, "What does all this old, dead, dry English history have to do with us?" The teacher's response was priceless. Here is how he describes it:

> Our teacher's eyes clouded over. She looked wistfully out the window and said, "In college, a group of us went to London for a month. The Tate Gallery, Parliament, St. Paul's—I saw it all. I felt the history, the glory. I fell in love with a college student from London. Someday, you'll go there too. I want you to love it as much as I loved it."[18]

What a wonderful image for hearing the words of Jesus as he envisions a different way of living in the world.

Ultimately, though, as helpful as analogies and images are, listeners need stories that enflesh what might otherwise remain vague concepts: mourning, peacemaking, and so forth. What do these qualities look like in real life? Alice Walker's short story, "The Welcome Table," is one example that comes to mind, a story that says as much about the marginalized and the church as it does about Jesus. It is the story of a woman, nameless and black, whom Walker describes as "the color of poor gray Georgia earth, beaten by king cotton and the extreme weather."

On this particular fine Sunday morning she starts off to worship at the big white church down the road, a church that is white in many ways. The good religious folks are shocked when she appears. The reverend kindly reminds her this is not her church, as if one could choose the wrong church. The young usher tries as well to persuade her to leave, but she has come to worship God. She settles into a pew near the back, noting to herself how cold it feels inside. Finally, the respectable ladies have had enough, and their husbands hurl the poor woman out onto the porch.

She is speechless. Only moments ago she was worshiping God. Then something happens. Listen to how Walker describes it: "She started to grin, toothlessly, with short giggles of joy, jumping about and slapping her hands on her knees. And soon it became apparent why she was so happy. For coming down the highway at a firm though leisurely pace was Jesus." She recognizes him from a picture in the Bible. As he approaches, he says, "Follow me," and without hesitation she joins him there on the road, although she has no idea where they are headed. She hums. She sings. She tells Jesus all about her troubles. He smiles. Listens and smiles, and the two of them walk on until the ground beneath their feet gives way to clouds and she is truly home![19]

Strategies for Preachers

David Buttrick addresses a common concern among many preachers when he asks, "How do we proclaim the Beatitudes? Preachers have preached on them in a bunch or, sometimes, drafted a series of sermons exploring them one by one." On the one hand, isolating them from each other over a period of weeks can lead to an atomistic theology. Preaching them in one sermon, on the other hand, can result in the preacher "moving down a list" rather than creating what Buttrick calls "a sense of visionary unity."[20]

Either way, we will definitely want to honor the text-segment's oral nature. As Warren Carter points out, the Beatitudes are divided into two groups of four (if we allow vv. 11 and 12 to serve as elaborations on v. 10). Both groups have thirty-six words. Both close with a reference to righteousness. In addition, the first four use alliteration in Greek, which one scholar has paraphrased: "Blessed are the poor in spirit, the plaintive, the powerless, and those who pine for righteousness."[21]

Sermon Possibilities

When reflecting on homiletical options for this week's text-segment, here are two options:
- Blessedness on the Unlikely
- A Call to Living Differently

Sample Sermon: The Beatitudes

We conclude this chapter not with a list of sermons, but a full sermon manuscript. The occasion was Sunday worship, September 23, 2001, less than two weeks after the terrorist attacks of 9/11. The setting was Pine Ridge Presbyterian Church in Kansas City, Missouri, where Jim Gordon serves as pastor. The task then, as always, was to bring a word relevant to the people and faithful to the church's Scriptures. Here is the sermon preached on that occasion.

"Blessed Are You…"——————————

Matthew 5:1–12

A Sermon by Mike Graves

Kathleen Norris is right. She notes that in times of catastrophe like these, "People still look to artists for *something,* maybe even hope."[22] You've seen all the memorials that sprang up in New York City, the sidewalk murals. People still look to artists in times like these. Even last Sunday's *Kansas City Star* contained a poem they commissioned of a local poet.

Norris goes on to tell the story about the Russian poet Anna Akhmatova standing in long lines outside a prison in St. Petersburg, wanting to leave letters and packages for loved ones who had been purged by Stalin. They didn't even know if their loved ones were alive. In the crowd, a woman recognized the poet and approached her. "Can you describe this?" she asked. "Can you describe this for us?" The poet hesitated, and with a wry smile replied, "I can!" And in the poems she went on to write, the people found some measure of comfort.

"Can you describe this?" The reporters try, and the political pundits too, even the preachers. It's why so many flocked to churches last Sunday, in many places more than went on Easter. "Can you describe this?" they ask. To be honest, I can't. I couldn't then either. My New Testament colleague and I were preparing for a class that fateful morning. We were to lead a discussion of Matthew 5, the Sermon on the Mount, the Beatitudes of Jesus. Somehow the words on the pages of our notes melted away, even the red letters of Jesus bled through the pages of our Bibles. We had nothing to say. The class was supposed to last an hour. We sat in silence for fifteen minutes, managed to mumble our way through a psalm, and left.

Who can describe this? It occurs to me now that maybe, just maybe, Jesus' words of blessing we had intended to discuss that day are just the words we needed to hear, and still need to hear. If Norris is right, that in times like these we turn to the artists and poets, what better piece of poetry than this? Maybe these are the words Jesus would utter again if asked to describe what happened and is still happening.

Of course, the church hasn't always regarded the poetic quality of Jesus' words here. Some have treated it like a list, like some kind of Scout manual—you know, a list of qualities to emulate if you want to earn your next merit badge. It's not a list. It's not a challenge. It's a word of blessing on those who are already poor in spirit, not those who are hoping to become that way some day. Do you hear it? "Blessed *are*..."

And that's another problem, that word *blessed*. What a strange word. You don't hear that word much anymore. Oh, sure someone sneezes in the narthex during friendship time: "Bless you." But that's a different word. This "bless*ed*" is different. In the syllabi for my classes there are warnings about turning work in late, but not a word about, "Blessed are those who are on time." "Blessed are the high school kids who don't smoke on church property." It's a strange word to our ears.

Some translators have suggested "happy." Happy is a good word, a happy word. It just sounds...happy. But *happy* is the kind of word that belongs at parties, with noisemakers and such. "Happy Birthday," "Happy Hanukkah," sure; but "Happy are those who mourn"? No, no!

Others have suggested "contented." "Contented are the poor in spirit." *Contented* is another good word, but when I hear that word, I picture our dog on the floor with a chew bone; or a family patting their full bellies on Thanksgiving afternoon. "Yeah, I think I'll have just one more piece of pie and then a nap." That's contentment; but "Contented are those who hunger and thirst..."?

More recently some scholars have suggested "congratulations." It's close to the Greek meaning here, but it doesn't quite work either. To be honest, it's hard to do better than "blessed," because *blessed* is a theological word, a word announcing God's favor on those who hear.

And that's another thing misunderstood about this beautiful passage: those who heard it. I don't know how you picture it, but listen to Matthew's description of Jesus' congregation from the end of chapter 4:

23 Jesus went throughout Galilee, teaching in their synagogues and proclaimingthe good news of the kingdom and curing every disease and every sickness among the people.

24 So his fame spread throughout all Syria, and they brought to him all the sick, those who were afflicted with various diseases and pains, demoniacs, epileptics, and paralytics, and he cured them.

25 And great crowds followed him from Galilee, the Decapolis, Jerusalem, Judea, and from beyond the Jordan (4:23–25).

Not exactly a "Who's Who of Temple Judaism." These were not the folks with resumes on file, looking to get ahead in the world. And so some scholars suggest that to really understand this passage, you have to appreciate these misfits gathered around Jesus.

Then again, maybe all you really have to do to understand these words of Jesus is find yourself poor in spirit, and sorrowful, and meek, and hungry, and thirsty, and, well, you get the idea. Somehow these words of blessing come alive in our moments of despair. Nora Gallagher tells about this friend of hers, a Jewish artist, who used to carry around these two pieces of paper in her pockets, one in each pocket. Everywhere she went, these two pieces of paper went with her. On the one was written, "I am dust and ashes," and on the other, "For me the world was created."[23] It is those who see themselves for who they really are who begin to understand Jesus' blessings.

Of course, there are those who argue that *understanding* Jesus' sermon is not really the point at all. It's not a discussion of how many gallons of jet fuel were involved or at what temperature steel melts. That was the discussion at the barbershop this week. No, these poetic words of Jesus are different. You don't so much try to understand them as to feel them. It's more about feeling the weight of Jesus' words as they fall bodily on you like showers of blessings on a parched soul.

Barbara Brown Taylor is a poet in her own right, a gifted Episcopalian priest and a marvelous preacher. She tells the story of visiting the Kachkar Mountains east of the Black Sea, between modern-day Turkey and Russia. A thousand years ago the region's Byzantine churches were monuments of beauty, "full of exquisite arches, frescos and stonework."[24] But Mongols conquered this kingdom in the 1200s, and it has since become predominately Muslim today. These once-great churches are now only museums at best. Many of them are abandoned among farmer's fields, the farmers having to pluck gargoyles out of the soil to plant their crops. Some of the former church sites serve as soccer fields, sheep pens, even garbage dumps. Their roofs are long gone, and so are the doors, the floors, the altars. However, in some places, remnants of early frescos remain.

Brown Taylor tells about this one fresco in particular that she came across: "half a face, with one wide eye looking right at you."[25] It's a fresco of the Christ with one arm raised in blessing. That's the picture here in Matthew 5—the Christ blessing the hurting, those whose lives, like abandoned churches, feel empty and hollow.

"Can you describe this?" That's what that woman asked the poet. "Can you describe this?" How can anyone describe what we have seen in the past ten-plus days? How can anyone describe such horror? I don't know what scene lives on in your memory, what video clip keeps replaying in your head. But picture two scenes for just a moment, and let them overlap if you can. Picture a mountain in ancient Palestine, with bearded peasants on makeshift crutches and frail women nursing babies. Picture them in the thousands, waiting to hear a word. And picture another mountain, a mountain of twisted steel and dust-filled air where thousands gather in utter despair. They post pictures in hopes that somehow...but they know.

And then hear the words, of how when Jesus saw the crowds, he went up the mountain and said, "Blessed are the poor in spirit. Blessed are those who mourn. Blessed are the meek. Blessed are those who hunger and thirst for righteousness. Blessed are the peacemakers. Blessed are the persecuted." Hear the words of Jesus, "Blessed are you... Blessed are you..." Amen.

CHAPTER 4

Matthew 14:22–33

Jesus Calms a Stormy Sea

Locating the Sermon

Twelfth Sunday after Pentecost (Year A)

If we have been preaching the lectionary's gospel passages, we have been in Matthew for ten weeks now and have even more than that ahead of us in the coming months. This is often good news for preachers who seem to reach their stride in a series of sermons from the same source, but for listeners it can be a different experience altogether. I remember our pastor before I went to seminary. He did not use the lectionary but loved to preach series. One series led us through Matthew's gospel. What started off as an exciting adventure soon become pedantic and plodding.

In the midst of our long stretch of Sundays from Matthew, we will want to seek creative ways to draw on previous insights, but without too much predictability. For the most part, each sermon will need to be able to stand on its own. In last week's reading we encountered a fully developed miracle story, Jesus feeding the multitudes. This week he calms a stormy sea. As we shall see, miracle stories present their own unique challenges for preachers and congregations alike. Of course, they also testify to God's power to provide and care for us. Before we consider preaching strategies, however, let us examine the text-segment in its ancient setting.

Understanding the Passage

Frequently this story in Matthew 14 appears in Bibles under a heading such as "Walking on Water," a phrase that has taken on a proverbial nature in our language, even beyond the walls of the church. To praise another person's ability, people may say, "She can walk on water." Or if a person is not as competent as she or he perceives, we might say, "He *thinks* he can walk on water." Walking on water has become a stereotypical phrase for someone who demonstrates extraordinary talents or skills. While there is an element of this aspect in Matthew 14:22–33 and its representation of Jesus, the narrative is also about how ordinary persons, caught in extraordinary circumstances, demonstrate faith by recognizing the true identity of Jesus.

How the Evangelist Crafted the Text-segment

Matthew 14:22–33 occurs in the midst of a Matthean context filled with both implicit and explicit questions about the identity of Jesus. Who is this one who causes the tetrarch Herod Antipas to tremble (14:1–12), who feeds thousands with only five loaves and two fishes (14:13–21), who uses waves as stepping stones (14:22–33), who heals without discrimination (14:34–36), and who causes Pharisees and scribes to leave the comfort of Jerusalem (15:1–9)? In presenting Jesus' identity, Matthew utilizes creative settings and succinct descriptions to illustrate the variety of ways people come to recognize Jesus. He also shows how people missed Jesus, and how sometimes, like Peter, they both recognize and misunderstand at the same time.

Verses 22–33 are the center focus that the author has creatively placed at the very heart of this identity-oriented context. The larger narrative frames with Herod Antipas (14:1–12) and the Pharisee/Scribes (15:1–9) illustrate how the authorities of that day, political and religious, struggled with the fame (honor) accruing to Jesus. In the immediate context, on either side of the walking on water scene, Jesus is surrounded by the crowds (14:13–21 and 14:34–36). These people are swarming Jesus for the two most basic needs in the first century: food and healing. The walking on water narrative in verses 22–33 narrows the readers' point of reference onto an intimate and initially terrifying encounter between Jesus and his disciples. And then, like a microscope which focuses on the last most critical object, the author narrows the reader's attention to just Jesus and Peter (vv. 18-32).

The following outline illustrates the way the author draws readers' attention to the climactic scene with Jesus and Peter.

> A   Herod's Questions about Jesus (14:1–12)
>> B   Jesus Feeding the Crowds (14:13–21)
>>> C   Jesus and His Disciples (14:22–27)
>>>> D   Jesus and Peter (14:28–32)
>>> C1   Jesus and His Disciples (14:32–33)
>> B1   Jesus Heals the Crowds (14:34–36)
> A1   Pharisees and Scribes Pose Questions to Jesus (15:1–9)

The above narrative structure is called a chiasm and helps a reader understand the fulcrum around which the author's other narratives circle.

Before evaluating more specifically the storm narrative in 14:22–33, a reader should explore the larger context and how the story of Herod Antipas (14:1–12) prepares the reader for what is to come. Herod Antipas is a representative of the political-kinship structures of the first-century world. He was one of the sons of Herod the Great and therefore belonged to the Herodian dynasty. Officially, by the decree of Rome, he was a tetrarch, ruler of a fourth of Palestine (as had been his brother, Archelaus, mentioned in chapter 1—though Archelaus's reign only lasted until 6 C.E., when the Romans removed him from power). Antipas had control over the geographical areas of Galilee and Perea for more than forty years (4 B.C.E. to 39 C.E.).[1] Matthew makes it clear that Herod Antipas's chief concern about Jesus stemmed from Jesus' increased fame (14:1). Antipas's anxious struggle was to try to identify who Jesus was. In the inner workings of Antipas's mind he solved this identity dilemma by settling on the fact that Jesus must be John the Baptist raised from the dead (v. 2).

The relationship of the Herod Antipas story with the focal passage in 14:22–33 may not at first be readily seen, but there are several points of connection. The first point is about identity and Antipas's attempt to pin down who Jesus is. Antipas does arrive at a conclusion; but, of course, it is incorrect. In 14:22–33, the disciples also struggle initially to identify Jesus when he approaches them in the midst of the storm, "It is a ghost!" (14:26). Just as Antipas was haunted by the specter of John the Baptist back from the dead, so are the disciples haunted by a specter (literally a *phantasma*). Unlike Antipas, however, the disciples do eventually recognize and correctly identify Jesus. Peter does it by calling Jesus "Lord" (14:28). When the wind ceases, all the disciples in the boat correctly identify and acknowledge Jesus as "Son of God" (v. 33).

Another connection to the Antipas story could easily be overlooked. Matthew has continued to portray how the reign of God represented by Jesus clashes with the kingdom represented by the Herodians/Romans.[2] Antipas was a son of Herod the Great; Jesus was/is the Son of God. Both of these sons represent very different kingdoms, and they each demonstrate their power in different ways. But who is the greater son? Who represents true authority and power?

These questions are answered in subtle ways in this narrative as a reader considers the geographical and historical setting of this event. Antipas founded the city of Tiberias between the years 17 and 20 c.e., and he named it for his patron, Emperor Tiberius. Antipas's wealth and power were demonstrated by establishing a city on *terra firma,* solid land. It was not just any city but the capital of his small geographical area. Jesus' reign and power, however, were demonstrated by his establishing control over the most chaotic of elements: the sea. In any comparison, the Son of God and his reign is superior to the son of Herod and his reign. No earthly ruler could establish authority over the sea. Perhaps it is significant that when the boat with the disciples and Jesus finally lands, the author specifically notes that the disciples and Jesus disembarked at Gennesaret (14:34–36). This area is a plain, 3.5 by 1.5 miles in area, on the northwest side of the Sea of Galilee between Tiberias and Capernaum. Perhaps the disciples and Jesus even land within sight of Tiberias—the city representing the "so-called" power of Herod Antipas.

If the Herod Antipas story prepares us for what is to come, the conflict with the Pharisees and scribes (15:1–9) reinforces and expands Jesus' extraordinary walking on the sea. While his power over the sea has demonstrated the identity of Jesus and his authority, the Pharisees and scribes are raising issues of his authority and power over the "traditions" (15:2).[3] Jesus, having been challenged by the Pharisees and scribes, as he had been challenged by the chaos of the sea, counter-challenges with a charge that the Pharisees and scribes are the ones violating the "traditions." He labels them as hypocrites, not for the first time (see 6:2, 5, 16; 7:5), and not for the last time (22:18; 23:13, 15, 23, 25, 27, 29). Since they do not respond to Jesus' challenge, they are silenced in the same way that the sea also was silenced by Jesus' authority.

If the outside frames of Herod Antipas and the Pharisees/ scribes stories demonstrate Jesus' authority and power, the immediate context of the crowds in 14:13–21 and 34–36 illustrate Jesus' patronage. In the first scene, Jesus provides food from the meager beginnings of five loaves and two fish (v. 19) for more than five thousand people. Jesus is a much more powerful patron than Herod Antipas, who is able to feed at his banquet only a small band of elites he has gathered around him (14:6). While the Pharisees are concerned about crossing purity boundaries related to eating with unwashed hands (15:2), Jesus has just demonstrated his patronage by healing without discrimination all who were sick and came to him (14:36).

Jesus had been touched and "polluted" by many diseased, and the Pharisees and scribes were concerned about hand-washing purity rituals.

All the stories on either side of 14:22–33 present a reader with a person who demonstrates kingly power and authority, who as a patron distributes the most basic needs of food and healing, and who stymies the religious authority and their worldview. But who is this man really? The answer to that question is found in verses 22–33 and in the echoes from the Hebrew Scriptures.

What the Text-segment Meant to the Community

The Hebrew Scriptures tradition in 14:22–33 would have rung in the ears of the original listeners. While we may be deaf to them today, the original audience would have recognized many of the cues within the narrative that illustrated Jesus' actions/authority as the characteristics of God. For example, in this narrative the author is continuing the theme of Jesus as one who has Moses-like qualities, but who is greater than Moses. Moses, who led God's people in the exodus from Egypt, may have been able to split the sea and walk across on dry land (Ex. 14), but Jesus is greater since he is able to walk *on* the sea. This exodus theme is revealed even earlier in the context of chapter 14 with Jesus' feeding of the crowds in verses 13–21. This episode is reminiscent of God's feeding of people in the wilderness (Ex. 16). Jesus is the one greater than Moses and the one who demonstrates the nurture and protective qualities of God.

Warren Carter also suggests that the exodus theme is found in Jesus extending his hand out and catching Peter as he is sinking into the sea (v. 31). He writes, "The phrase 'stretch out one's hand' can also signify acts of danger from which humans need saving by God's outstretched hand (Gen. 3:22; 22:10–11). So in *extending his hand* to save Peter, Jesus again does what God does."[4] The saving power of Jesus is extended to disciples in the boat and in the next healing scene (vv. 34–36).

Jesus' ability to walk on the sea draws the reader's attention to the creation account in Genesis in which God creates the waters and has control over them. Jesus demonstrates the same type of control over nature, specifically the chaos of the sea, that God does. For the author of Matthew, the Son has attributes like the Father—or, in more colloquial terms, he is "a chip off the old block."

One final echo from the Hebrew Scriptures is also prominent in this narrative. When Jesus appears on the sea, the disciples are fearfully thinking that an apparition is coming toward them. Matthew writes, "They were terrified" (literally, "stirred up," *taparasso*). The external storm paled in comparison to the "stirred up" storm they were experiencing internally. Jesus identifies himself and in the process calms the disciples' internal storm by saying, "Take heart; it is I" (14:27). Literally, Jesus has uttered the phrase, "I am" (*ego eimi*). This was the great hidden name of God revealed to Moses at the burning bush (Ex. 3:14). Instead of a fiery bush in a desert, however, here is a person in the midst of a sea who utters the divine name. Will Peter and the disciples, as Moses did, recognize the theophany they are encountering? For Matthew the answer is yes. By the time Jesus calms both the sea and the disciples' fears, the disciples recognize Jesus for who he is. They worship, an action reserved only for Yahweh, but they worship Jesus and declare, "Truly you are the Son of God" (v. 35).

One of the purposes of this narrative, especially if the above chiasm is considered, highlights the disciple Peter.[5] Also, in comparison with the parallel account of this narrative in Mark 6:45–56, one of the most obvious differences is that no detailed story about Peter's attempted water walking is included in Mark's account.[6] Only Matthew expands this story to include this unique story about Peter's actions.

Several interesting observations can be made about Peter and his watery encounter with Jesus. First is the title by which Peter addresses Jesus. In both verse 28 and in verse 30, Peter calls Jesus "Lord" (*kyrie*). Luke Timothy Johnson notes that the author of Matthew is very precise and careful when using the title Lord.[7] He writes, "Jesus is never called Teacher by the disciples, the afflicted, or those coming to faith in him. The disciples (8:25; 14:28; 16:22; 17:4; 18:21) and those coming to faith in Jesus (8:2, 6, 8; 9:28; 15:22, 25, 27; 17:15; 20:30) always call him Lord (but see 26:18)."[8] Matthew was seeking to set his community over against any group that would understand Jesus only as an earthly rabbi/teacher. For Matthew and his community, Jesus was much more.

With the honorific title of Lord on his lips, Peter is initially portrayed as one of faith who recognizes Jesus. Recognition and faith culminate in Peter's petition to leave the boat and to come to Jesus on the water. Jesus grants this petition with one word, "Come" (v. 29). The initial steps of success on the sea, however, turn into flopping and floundering when Peter saw the wind (v. 30).[9] Peter's fear sinks him, and Jesus has to rescue him. Now it is Jesus' turn to give a title to Peter: "You of little faith" (v. 31).

This title is not a first for the disciples; they have been chided before for their puny faith. In another boat-caught-in-the-storm scene (8:23–27), Jesus admonishes all the disciples by saying, "Why are you afraid, you of little faith" (v. 26). This narrative in 8:23–27 ends on a more negative note than 14:22–33. In 8:27 the disciples are left questioning, "What sort of man is this?" In 14:33, however, the disciples may still have little faith, but it is growing. They now acknowledge what sort of man Jesus is: He is the Son of God.

Interpretive Summary

A common element of Jesus' condemnatory phrase about "little faith" in both of these stories is fear. Peter's fear in 14:30 caused him to sink, and the disciples' fear caused them to wake Jesus in 8:25–26. The wedding together of faith and fear is a natural characteristic for Matthew. He was writing to a community experiencing its own personal storm. The community of Judean-Christians was being expelled from the secure and known boundaries of their synagogue roots. Johnson summarizes it in this way: "Hostility between messianist and non-messianist Jews grew more fierce after that point [the fall of the temple] and reached a crystallization in the *Birkat-ha-minim,* which brought curses on heretics and made it impossible for Christians to pray in synagogues from this point on."[10] It is a fearful thing to lose one's foundation and to feel like a piece of flotsam and jetsam on the sea. No doubt Matthew was hoping to encourage his community to persevere in the face of the difficult times they were experiencing and would experience.

The boat is mentioned prominently in verses 22–33 and carries more import than just a prop or scene-setting device for this narrative.[11] David Garland notes that biblical interpreters through the centuries have understood the boat to symbolize the church.[12] As a symbol for the church, the boat highlights a place of security for disciples, especially when Jesus is present. Note that Matthew illustrates the protection quality of the boat-church by describing how the winds ceased when Jesus and Peter "got into the boat" (v. 32). Frederick Buechner writes that even in some church architecture today one can find the boat-church motif prominent: "The nave is the central part of the church from the main front to the chancel… It takes its name from the Latin *navis,* meaning ship, one reason being that the great vaulted roof looks rather like an inverted keel."[13]

Preaching the Passage

The Familiar and Unfamiliar

If ever there were a passage of Scripture full of the familiar and unfamiliar, this is it. As for the familiar: boats, storms, waves–these are the things of ordinary life, at least for those who now live or grew up near water. Even for landlubbers, the images are familiar enough, thanks to literature, television, and movies. As for the unfamiliar, try a story in which Jesus walks on water, commands one of his disciples to do the same with mixed results, and calms a storm. Landlubber or experienced sailor, this is strange territory!

Every preacher will immediately acknowledge that when Sunday comes, some kind of explanation will be in order. It is a miracle story. What do we do with miracles? Explain them? Explain them away? Defend them? What do we do? In part, of course, the answer depends on our theology. Still, if we understand how miracle stories functioned as a literary form in the first century, we may have a better idea of how to approach the subject.

Even though Matthew offers a wide range of miracle stories (from exorcisms to rescue stories like this one), all of them have this in common: the point is not so much about the miracle as the story told through it—miracle *stories*.[14] In other words, the evangelist was not nearly so interested in the fact that Jesus could walk on water (that is a given in the text and apparently in Matthew's community) as he was in what such a thing says to the church. In this case, if the point were simply about the claim, "Jesus can walk on water," the text-segment would be much more detailed about just how he did it. When Jesus walks on water, does he step over the waves or push on through them? Apparently, that's not Matthew's agenda. In actuality, the text-segment spends very little time on the actual miracle and considerably more space on the significance of the story in which the miracle is found.

While scholars note the stress on the story, not so much on the miracle; and while preachers, too, may be quick to agree, listeners are a different case altogether. The problem facing us this coming Sunday is not how *we* feel about the miracles in New Testament scholarship. Not hardly. No, the dilemma is what to do with it in terms of *listeners'* expectations. In my experience, most preachers address it in one of two ways. Some (maybe most?) tackle the issue head on, and early in the sermon at that. For instance, the first words out of Michael Hough's mouth in a sermon on this passage are as follows: "For a proper understanding of our Gospel story, we need to go back to the beginning of the Bible, to the opening verses of Genesis. There we find the author presenting a clear theological understanding of our human existence."[15]

Over the next few paragraphs (several minutes of the sermon) Hough details the importance of stormy seas as a backdrop for this miracle story.

When I (Mike Graves) have preached from this passage, I, too, have sensed the need for some measure of explanation, but sought to address it more narratively. For instance, after beginning with the opening scene from the movie *Amistad,* one in which a storm occurs at sea, I briefly allude to something that happened at Blockbuster when my wife and I tried to rent a copy:

> The guy at the counter said, "You know, they say that the movie isn't accurate historically." "Yeah, that's what I've heard." I couldn't really tell if knowing that had ruined the movie for him or not. One of those, "If it's not history, it's just a story!" kind of responses.

I then proceed to note how some people call stories like this one a myth, adding, "I don't know what you think of when you hear that word, but I like what Kathleen Norris writes. She says a myth is a 'story that you know must be true the first time you hear it.' Or there's the definition a five-year-old shared with her: a myth is a story that may or may not be true on the outside, but you know it's true on the inside."[16]

As for the story told inside this text-segment, the evangelist clearly signals a message to a struggling church. Douglas Hare writes, "It is perhaps for the sake of his readers that Matthew writes 'those in the boat' where we expect him to have 'the disciples' (v. 33). Not just the apostles but all believers are in the endangered ship and dependent on their savior."[17] As modern-day preachers we will need to inform listeners of the evangelist's intended message for the church in every age.

In addition, while most seminary graduates immediately pick up on the chaotic waters of Genesis that stand behind this story, as well as the more subtle allusions to the divine name, "I am," most listeners will miss these things. As for the latter, it doesn't help that the Greek "I am" is translated somewhat awkwardly into the English expression, "It is I." It makes Jesus sound like one of the three musketeers: "It is I!" Preachers must decide how direct or narrative to be in their teaching/preaching from the pulpit. The classroom settings of Christian education afford opportunities that worship settings often do not.

Making Connections

If indeed the text-segment says something to Christ's church caught in the midst of storms, most listeners are ready to hear such a message. Pick up any copy of *The Christian Century*, or even a typical newspaper, and stories of church scandals and the like are commonplace. Debates about sexuality and differing views on war (usually in that order) make the headlines regularly. The church is most definitely in trouble.

The trouble for the preacher, however, is more complicated than that. In this text-segment Matthew stresses not internal conflict (as we find in Acts and some of Paul's epistles), bickering between those on the boat, but the wind and waves battering the church from without. But today, in most North American contexts, the church is rarely battered from without. Politicians get elected to office quoting Scripture and then get sworn in with one hand on a Bible.

This is not always the case, of course. Some churches do indeed take blows for their prophetic stand in a community, challenging social injustices where they see them. Here is a word for the struggling church: "Christ is with us; the one named Emmanuel, God with us, will be present in our struggles." What a wonderful word of encouragement, which as Carol Norén rightly notes is the most appropriate word because the story is not nearly so much about Peter or us, as it is about the faithfulness of Christ toward us.[18]

More common than we might like to think, however, are actual persecutions of the church in other parts of the world.

Unfortunately, as preachers we rarely think in terms of solidarity with the church universal. We read text-segments about persecution and wonder what the other lectionary passages might have to offer. "Persecution? We're sponsoring a car wash this week for the youth's mission trip." Never mind the fact that the place to which the youth are journeying has often witnessed persecution of believers.

So the preacher can speak a word to the local congregation in the midst of trials and travails, but the wise preacher can, from time to time, also speak a word on behalf of brothers and sisters in other locales who know suffering to a far greater degree than we. This is a form of witnessing, bearing testimony to what we have seen.

A Stormy Sea: Stories for Sermons

In his fascinating book *How to Read Literature Like a Professor,* Thomas Foster claims that in Western literature if there is a meal portrayed, communion is intended. The same for characters coming out of water, the image being baptism.[19] While some might question the veracity of such a claim, I suspect Foster is right, because as he goes on to note, authors are very intentional about settings. And perhaps the same can be said for storms in literature. It is for good reasons, indeed, that authors include such scenes. They are highly symbolic, signifying struggles of great magnitude.

In the case of this text-segment, the storm occurs at sea. It might be wise, then, that we begin our brainstorming of possible sermon material with images and stories related to storms at sea. When I preached on this passage, I thought about Frederick Buechner's novel *The Storm,*[20] and a watercolor by Winslow Homer, "The Coming Storm." I also thought about the storm scene in my all-time favorite movie, *Places in the Heart,* a storm that shows no discrimination. As I mentioned above, I also thought of Steven Spielberg's *Amistad,* as well as my own experiences growing up on the Gulf coast of Texas with all its storms.

It was these latter two sources—the image of storms from my childhood while fishing with my dad as well as the movie *Amistad*—that played the largest part of contemporary imagery in the sermon I preached. Most preachers will be able to recall storm experiences of their own, even if they didn't occur at sea. Recalling such personal experiences will heighten the ability to describe what all people have experienced at one time or another, the lack of control and the frightful worry associated with storms. With good reasons the World Council of Churches has taken for its icon a storm-tossed ship, but with a cross as the ship's mast.

But just because the text-segment occurs at sea does not mean the sermon must use identical imagery. Barbara Brown Taylor retells the biblical narrative in some detail, after which she includes three contemporary analogies, only one of which is water-related:

> Even if you have never tried to walk on water, you know how he felt. Maybe you were crossing a stream on a fallen log, inching your way across its rough, rounded surface, doing just fine until you looked down at the rushing water below you and got frightened, and lost your balance, and had to drag yourself the rest of the way by the seat of your pants.[21]

She describes similar scenarios about learning to ride a bicycle or addressing a crowd, recalling how initial elation gave way to fear and failure. Only then does she remind us that the same Jesus who told Peter to come is the one who rescued him, and, by extension, the one who rescues us today.[22]

Sermon Possibilities

Having examined this text-segment, here are three sermon possibilities:
- God's Saving Power over Chaos and Persecution
- The Christ Who Is Always with Us

- Remembering Our Brothers and Sisters around the World

A Sermon Sampler

As samples, let us consider five very different sermons on this story of Jesus calming the storm:

Fred B. Craddock, "Faith and Fear," in *The Cherry Log Sermons* (Louisville: Westminster John Knox Press, 2001), 31–35.

Mike Graves, "Followed by the Sun!" *Review and Expositor* 99 (Winter 2002): 91–96.

Michael Hough, "For Those Who Trust in God," in *Best Sermons* 5, ed. James W. Cox (New York: HarperSanFrancisco, 1992), 86–92.

Carol Marie Norén, "Christ–Beside Us in the Storm," in *Pulpit Resource* 27 (July-September 1999): 23–26.

Barbara Brown Taylor, "Saved by Doubt," in *The Seeds of Heaven: Sermons on the Gospel of Matthew* (Louisville: Westminster John Knox Press, 2004), 55–60.

CHAPTER 5

Matthew 21:1–11

Jesus Enters Jerusalem

Locating the Sermon

Palm/Passion Sunday (Year A)

Although the story of Jesus' entry into Jerusalem comes around every year, Matthew's version is only one of three the church hears. Since John's gospel makes cameo appearances every spring, the Lenten/Easter season can be somewhat confusing for us as preachers. For instance, while the transfiguration story comes from Matthew (17:1–9), as does the Lectionary text for the first week of Lent (4:1–11), the next four Sundays come from the Fourth Gospel. A similar thing happens after Easter, when Matthew's account of the resurrection (28:1–10) then gives way to eight weeks of text-segments from John and Luke, before the many Sundays after Pentecost return us to Matthew.

Confusion is also associated with the traditional designation "Palm Sunday," which in recent years has become more commonly referred to as "Passion Sunday," and rightly so. For starters, while Matthew and Mark do mention "branches from the trees" spread out on the road (Mt. 21:8; Mk. 11:8 reads "leafy branches"), Luke makes no mention of palms or branches of any kind. More importantly, the traditional title is usually accompanied by the designation "triumphal entry," which misses the irony. Matthew's use of Zechariah 9 omits the reference to "triumphant and victorious is he." A carpenter-rabbi trotting into town on a donkey is hardly triumphal.

As for the story of Jesus' entry into Jerusalem, perhaps the biggest obstacle is the tendency toward harmonizing Matthew's account with those of the other gospels. So before we consider how we might go about preaching the text-segment, let us once again ponder the passage in its ancient setting.

Understanding the Passage

If we choose to retain the "Triumphal Entry" title, we must do so with the greatest sense of irony. This entry by Jesus into Jerusalem is unlike any other triumphant processional familiar to first-century people. If it is a triumph, then we need to accept Matthew's definition of a triumph. It is not an imperial Roman grand propaganda parade heaping accolades on a king/warrior for the successful incorporation of another province into the empire that was Rome. It was a parade, certainly, but not that type of parade. The sad-eyed man riding into Jerusalem on a donkey that day was leading a funeral parade—his own.

How the Evangelist Crafted the Text-segment

Matthew 21:1–11 occurs at a strategic turning point in the plotting and timing of the gospel. This episode initiates the start of the passion narrative. As Paul Meyer states, "The Passion Narrative in Matthew as in Mark clearly has two beginnings. In the narrower sense, the final events of Jesus' life are set in motion at Matthew 26:1 (see Mark 14:1) with the decision of the authorities in Jerusalem to move against him... Yet in the broader reach of the Gospel, there is another beginning when Jesus first enters Jerusalem."[1] In a very real sense, this week's passage begins the march toward the passion of Jesus. In this march Jesus will continue to deliver parables, teach, heal, provide prophetic words and actions, and engage in frequent debates with religious authorities—all typical acts associated with Jesus throughout the gospel of Matthew. However, with Jesus' entry into Jerusalem, to use another triumphant image from the ancient world, he has "crossed the Rubicon." For Matthew, Jesus' words and actions in 21:1—25:46 are critical, penultimate events that will ultimately provoke the arrest, trial, and crucifixion of Jesus in 26:1—27:66.

If the larger context of this passage is set within the passion of Jesus, the immediate context for 21:1–11 provides background for understanding the specific issues within these verses. The scene immediately before Jesus' entry into Jerusalem recounts the petition from and healing of two blind men (20:29–34). The most readily noticeable connection is the repeated use of the title "Son of David" for Jesus (20:30, 31). The blind men's shouts had barely subsided before the shouts of "Hosanna to the Son of David" come from the pilgrimage crowd in 21:9. This title, along with Jesus' unusual mode of transportation into Jerusalem, evoked a question about his identity from the Jerusalem crowd (v. 10). The reverberation of the title Son of David continues into 21:14–17 when the religious leaders display indignation regarding the public proclamation of Jesus' so-called lineage.

It is difficult for an interpreter to miss that "Son of David" is a prominent theme for understanding the various reactions to Jesus' appearance in Jerusalem in 21:1–11. As Meyer notes, "David was a generator of symbolic meaning."[2] To mention the name of David was to generate powerful images: the founder of Jerusalem, the power of military strength, the deliverer from oppression, the provider of justice, and "the standing ('glory') of God himself among all the peoples of the earth."[3] To declare that Jesus was the *Son* of David also evoked the powerful social institution of kinship. In the first-century world, kinship was the way to establish one's family group, and the family group "defines the present, is rooted in the past, and expresses future potentialities."[4] Matthew initiates the kinship connection with David at the very beginning of the gospel with the genealogy (1:1–17). By placing David as the apical ancestor, the one from whom all traits flow, Matthew provides a perspective by which to examine and interpret all of Jesus' actions and words.[5] The Davidic seed Matthew plants in 1:1, he brings to full bloom with the crowds' cries of recognition in 21:9.

Ironically, the blind men who shouted the title "Son of David" were able to "see" the kingship—kinship represented by Jesus—when others missed it. The need for opened eyes about Jesus' identity will be a recurring metaphor in the coming chapters. Who and what will people perceive when they see Jesus coming into Jerusalem on a donkey? The city crowd puts its confused perceptions this way, "Who is this?" (21:10). This confusion causes a reader to wonder why the people of Jerusalem could not see as clearly as the blind men of Jericho. The blindness that seems to darken all the people of Jerusalem is epitomized in Jesus' lament over the city, "For I tell you, you will not see me again until you say, 'Blessed is the one who comes in the name of the Lord'" (23:39).

The scenes following 21:1–11, specifically, the cleansing of the temple (vv. 12–13), and challenges to Jesus about his origins as Son of David (vv. 14–17), also throw light on this passage. The status of Jesus is climatically acknowledged in verse 11 with his role as a prophet. Jesus, by his action of riding into Jerusalem on a donkey, has already performed one prophetic action, but this action may not be recognized or understood. In verses 12–13, however, the prophetic action in the temple precinct cannot be overlooked or ignored. Like the prophets from the past who found symbolic ways to protest against temple corruption and complacency, Jesus' cleansing of the temple demonstrates his lineage not only as "Son of David," but also as prophet. Perhaps Matthew is attempting to combine the two roles of king and prophet. Some New Testament writers explicitly combine a Davidic kingly role with a Davidic prophetic role. For example, in the Acts of the Apostles, David is clearly portrayed as a prophet: "Since he [David] was a prophet, he knew that God had sworn with an oath to him that he would put one of his descendants on this throne. Foreseeing this, David spoke of the resurrection of the Messiah" (Acts 2:30–31a).

Just as the cries of the blind men raise the issue of Jesus' Davidic origin, so the voices of children raise it in 21:14–17. In verse 15, the children mimic the cries of the crowds and shout, "Hosanna to the Son of David!" The source of this proclamation should not trouble the chief priests and scribes; it is only the babbling of children in the street. Honor is at stake, however, since the designation of Jesus as from the lineage of David is a public announcement. Therefore, the religious leaders challenge Jesus over these childish cries (21:16). Jesus responds with a counter-challenge, "Have you never read, 'Out of the mouths of infants and nursing babes, / you have prepared praise for yourself'?" which is from Psalm 8:2. By Jesus' response, he acknowledges that the words of the children are true: he is the Son of David. By the leaders' lack of response, they are revealed as poor interpreters of Scripture and poor judges of Jesus' identity. In other words, they are shamed.

All four gospels include Jesus' entry into Jerusalem (Mk. 11:1–10; Lk. 19:28–38; Jn. 12:12–16). When Matthew's account is compared with these parallels, a few interesting points are highlighted. For example, the Son of David theme becomes even more pronounced since it is not found in the other accounts. Matthew also includes a scriptural fulfillment citation from Zechariah 9:9. Both Mark and Luke have no reference to the prophet Zechariah; however, surprisingly, the gospel of John also uses an abbreviated form of this citation (Jn. 12:15). The synoptics all follow the plot sequence of Jesus' first sitting on the donkey and only then of the crowds giving adoration and recognition. In the gospel of John, however, the sequence is reversed. First, the crowds greet Jesus and proclaim him blessed as the one "who comes in the name of the Lord—the King of Israel" (Jn. 12:13b). Only then does Jesus sit on the donkey and ride.

Not surprisingly, one of the significant differences between the accounts is how Jesus is identified. In both Luke and John,

Jesus is explicitly identified as king (Lk. 19:38; Jn. 12:13). In Mark, the focus, while not taken directly off of Jesus, shifts to the theme of the kingdom that he is bringing: "Blessed is the coming kingdom of our ancestor David" (Mk. 11:10). As noted above, Matthew uses the theme of Son of David, and this theme provides an oblique way to highlight Jesus' kingship. It may be Matthew's way of blunting the edge of a sword into a plowshare, for Jesus will not be the type of militaristic messiah some expected.

As Matthew begins this crucial section of his passion narrative, he uses laserlike precision to draw the reader's attention rapidly to Jerusalem, then to Bethphage, and ultimately to the Mount of Olives. Jesus' association with mountains is well known in Matthew.[6] Most of these mountains are unnamed or have been conveniently named by modern interpreters, e.g., Mount of Beatitudes or the Mount of Transfiguration. Here, however, is a mount with a specific name: Mount of Olives. This specificity provides a reader not only with a geographical context but also a theological context. As Warren Carter notes, "The Mount of Olives is a place of eschatological judgment and salvation in Zech. 14:4."[7] For Jesus to come to this place would carry the same symbolic *gravitas* as Martin Luther King Jr.'s selection of the Lincoln Memorial for the culmination of the March on Washington, D.C., in 1963. Among the many memorials in Washington, D.C., the Lincoln Memorial carried the symbolism of freedom, liberation, and equality. In the same way, the Mount of Olives figured in the history and tradition of Israel. It was a place pregnant with a symbolic significance for the past of Israel and its hoped-for future.

Matthew carefully composes and balances two distinct sections within 21:1–11. The first part is composed of verses 1–7 and describes Jesus' instructions to his disciples about preparing for his entry into Jerusalem. The second part in verses 8–11 illustrates the varied responses of the crowds to the appearance of Jesus.

In verses 1–7, the disciples are portrayed with one major characteristic: obedience. Jesus tells the disciples to "go, untie, and bring," the donkey and its foal. In the process, they were to let no one stand in the way of completing this mission. The disciples ask no questions, but "went and did as Jesus had directed them" (v. 6). Their actions are reminiscent of Joseph, who speaks not a word in the birth narratives but does all that he is instructed (1:18–25; 2:13–15, 19–23). The disciples demonstrate a type of righteousness characterized by the actions of obedience.

In 21:8–11 a sensitive reader will note two different crowds with two different responses to Jesus.[8] The first crowd is composed of pilgrims making its way into Jerusalem to participate in the Passover. Estimates suggest that a festival such as Passover might have drawn into Jerusalem (a city of appropriately 50,000) about 125,000 pilgrims.[9] These are the ones who proclaim Jesus as Son of David. The second group is represented by the crowd of Jerusalem. This group does not know what to make of Jesus and asks: "Who is he?" (v. 10). The pilgrims give the optimistic and partially correct reply, "This is the prophet Jesus from Nazareth in Galilee" (v. 11).

Although both groups are Judeans, they represent two very different ways to view their current situation. Many of those from outlying areas such as Galilee, Perea, Iturea, and Trachonitis would be wishing for new rulers instead of Herod Antipas or Herod Philip. Perhaps even more, they wished for the removal of the occupiers, the Romans, as represented by Pontius Pilate and the legions. The crowd of Jerusalem, on the other hand, a city dominated by the priestly class and elites, would side with the Romans and understand any outside agitators as a threat to the status quo. As William Herzog observes, "A great deal has been made about the fickle nature of the crowd that greeted Jesus with acclamations when he entered the city...and then turned into a frenzied mob screaming for his crucifixion... The crowd is vacillating only if it is the same crowd, a very dubious assumption."[10] It is clear that two different crowds with two different responses to Jesus were jostling together in these verses with their opinions and questions.

A third group, although not mentioned in verses 1–11, was certainly interested observers of any pilgrim mob flocking into Jerusalem: the Romans. Even if their Latin ears could not comprehend the words about kingship in the pilgrims' songs, they could certainly detect that the songs were not sung with hollow and apathetic voices but with gusto and bravado. Also, it would not escape their attention that the songs were directed toward a specific man riding on a donkey. Romans were always wary of festival crowds. During the numerous Judean festivals Pontius Pilate, prefect of Rome and administrator of this sub-province of Syria from 26 to 36 C.E., would have to leave his pleasurable seaside resort city of Caesarea and come into Jerusalem with cohorts of soldiers to insure order. Typically during the festivals unrest and agitation against Rome could be flamed to its greatest intensity. One can imagine a semi-interested Roman soldier sitting atop Jerusalem's walls picking his teeth with one hand and shielding his eyes from the sun with the other as he watched this parade representing one more would-be king of Judea who could easily and quickly be dethroned from his little donkey.

What the Text-segment Meant to the Community

In verses 4 and 5, Matthew interrupts Jesus' actions and the disciples' obedient response to his instructions by presenting to his readers the scriptural foundation for Jesus' directions and soon-to-be actions. As typical of Matthew's style, he invokes the Hebrew Scriptures as a witness for what happens in the life and ministry of Jesus. For Jesus' entry into Jerusalem on a donkey, Matthew utilizes two biblical citations: Isaiah 62:11 and Zechariah 9:9. One should note Matthew carefully shaped these citations for inclusion in this context. For example, instead of "Rejoice greatly daughter of Zion" as found in the beginning of Zech 9:9, Matthew uses Isaiah 62:11 as the introduction: "Tell the daughter of Zion"—perhaps because the daughter of Zion, Jerusalem, is not welcoming and rejoicing in Jesus' coming. Also, the emphasis on telling and proclamation is one that will be a model quality for disciples in the reign of God, as seen in Jesus' instructions to his disciples in 28:20.

Zechariah 9:9 is taken from the context of chapters 9—14 in Zechariah. These chapters highlight God's conquering of enemies and the restoration of Israel. In a comparison with the quote of Zechariah 9:9, Matthew's version omits the phrase emphasizing the king coming "triumphant and victorious." With Matthew's omission of these particular characteristics, he can better emphasize the most prominent characteristic retained from Zechariah 9:9, a king who is humble.

Interpretive Summary

Jesus' humble entry is not typical for a Greco-Roman triumphal procession. In an imperial procession, nothing was low-key, subtle, or left to chance. While no video exists to illustrate for a contemporary interpreter the characteristics of a triumphal procession, both literary and archaeological evidence presents enormous amounts of information about the nature of imperial parades of triumph. As Peter Holliday writes, "If military victory was the most important way for Roman aristocrats to secure *laus* and *gloria,* the triumph awarded for a successful military commander, Roman society's most spectacular and esteemed celebration, provided unparalleled means for fashioning an auspicious public image."[11] Virgil's *Aeneid* and Livy's *History* provide frequent descriptions of the grand pageantry associated with a triumph. One has only to observe the still-standing Arch of Titus with the triumphant Titus in a *quadriga,* a chariot pulled by four horses, to capture only one frozen moment of what such a choreographic procession must have been like. In Matthew's portrayal of Jesus, however, his definition of "triumphant" is a parody or lampooning of the Greco-Roman procession—no *quadriga,* no spoils, no parading of captives, no elites basking in the reflected glory.

One other specific way that Jesus' triumph can be seen as a parody of the Roman is in his action in the temple. In a typical Roman triumph, the final act of the procession had a religious element that culminated with the *triumphator* going to a temple, often the Temple of Jupiter Optimus Maximus, and offering a portion of the spoils (*spolia*) of victory.[12] In Matthew, Jesus' procession also climaxes in the temple, but it is not to present spoils of war/victory but to decry the corruption and spoiling of the temple (21:13). What function may this parody or lampooning serve for Matthew? Walter Wink provides a helpful insight: "The Powers That Be literally stand on their dignity. Nothing depotentiates them faster than deft lampooning. By refusing to be awed by their power, the powerless are emboldened to seize the initiative, even where structural change is not immediately possible."[13] Matthew presents, ironically, a man on a donkey surrounded by an army of believing peasants conquering the Roman Empire.

Preaching the Passage

The Familiar and Unfamiliar

If the story of Jesus' entry into Jerusalem is well-known, we can probably assume that what is known is more a caricature than an accurate reading of Matthew's account. Easter pageants portray Jesus on a donkey (no one dares to do anything with Matthew's *two* animals, and who can blame them?), with the whole city gladly shouting Hosanna (never mind that the cry, "Save us now," may have degenerated into a half-hearted "Hurrah" in Jesus' time), only to have the same cast members shout, "Crucify him!" later in the drama (with the pageant making no distinction between "the whole city" [v. 10] and "the crowds" [v. 11] as Matthew carefully portrays it).

The preacher must also deal with the local congregation's own traditions associated with this Sunday in their worship. In many places children march around the sanctuary with palms or balloons, or both, waving and shouting. What a happy time! No pathos. No irony. Nothing of the Suffering Servant. Perhaps the biggest obstacle is overcoming all this tradition—not necessarily playing "the Grinch who stole Lent," but wading through a well-established *gestalt* associated with the day.

Making Connections

Even if we have seen movies set in ancient Rome and the like, watched military leaders striding into various cities on the big screen, most of us are still not familiar with such pageantry. Not really. Even World War II images of allied forces liberating part of Europe are removed from our experiences today. So what are we to do with an even more ancient story of Jesus entering Jerusalem? Is this one of those texts in which the church simply relates what happened long ago, but without any relevant message for today?

What we in North America, particularly the United States, often fail to realize is how frequently similar scenes are enacted in other parts of the world. Military dictatorships still parade before the masses as a show of power. Even our own military enacts fly-overs, awesome displays of power designed to thrill a gathered crowd.

No, it's not that triumphal entries are all that foreign to our experience so much as the irony in Matthew's version is so often missed. Preachers don't rely much on irony these days. Maybe they never did. Comedians use irony. Whole episodes of *Seinfeld* depend on irony. But we preachers rarely use it, or its cousin satire. I remember hearing a minister preaching at the ordination of a former student, one of those grand occasions in the life of churches but typically without much fanfare or attendance. He began his sermon by noting how much trouble he had getting there that day. "I could hardly find a place to park. It's amazing how many people attend ordination services on any given Sunday rather than sit home watching football or napping the afternoon away." This seasoned minister recognized the value of satire.

Matthew's account of Jesus' entry into Jerusalem is one of the ways he pokes fun at Rome's dominance in the ancient world; and, as Warren Carter notes, in this story Jesus makes "an ass out of Rome."[14] Seeking to connect this ancient story to our own situation, the preacher, functioning as a prophet of irony, could look for similar connections. What are the powers that need to be challenged? What shows of might could be contrasted with the gentle ways of Jesus?

In addition to the irony, we do not want to ignore the narrative quality of this text-segment, similar to so many others in Matthew. Novelist Ron Hansen tells the story of his experience as a little boy at Sunday Mass in Omaha. The priest began reading one of the many familiar stories from one of the gospels. "The sentences were sure and predictable to me; I felt I was finally their audience; and I realized with a good deal of wonder that the Gospels were like those children's books that my mother or sisters would read to me over and over again."[15] Hansen means by that, not some sense of fiction as opposed to fact, but the renewing power of such stories, the familiarity by which the gospel stories get into our bones when heard over and over.

When we preach from such familiar stories we will want to avoid taking them for granted. They need unpacking, to be sure. At the same time, we will want to allow room for listeners to revel in the story itself. A retelling of Jesus' entry into Jerusalem, along with contemporary connections, is a powerful thing in the hands of God and in our mouths.

Sermon Possibilities

There are multiple options for preachers as they explore Scripture. Here are three to ponder:
- Speaking Truth to the Powers
- The Humility of Jesus
- Passion Sunday, Not Palms

Sample Sermon: Entering Jerusalem Today

Instead of considering some possible stories and sample sermons in isolation, let us look at a full-blown sermon first preached in 2005, at Saint Andrew Christian Church, in Olathe, Kansas.

"On a Scale of 1 to 10"

A Sermon by Mike Graves

Let's face it; in the life of the church, it doesn't get any bigger than these next eight days—Holy Week and Easter. Nothing any bigger than that! Maundy Thursday, the day we remember Jesus' commandment (or mandate) to love one another the way he loved us, wrapping a towel about himself and washing the disciples' dirty feet. Whew! On a scale of 1–10, Maundy Thursday's probably a 200, something like that. It blows you away. And what about Good Friday, originally called God Friday? Jesus crucified and hung out to dry, ignored by all, apparently even God. On a scale of 1–10, Good Friday has to be about a 250! As for that Saturday, I have no idea how to rank it, the silence of God, the broken hearts of Jesus' followers. And then comes Easter, the highest and holiest day of them all. On a scale of 1–10, Easter is about a 300—okay, maybe 3,000, maybe 3 billion. Beyond all expectations, the Son of God is raised from the dead; back from the dead. On a scale of 1–10, there is no scale when it comes to the day of resurrection.

Which brings us to today, Palm Sunday, the beginning of Holy Week, the day when we recall Jesus' entry into Jerusalem. I was recalling a particular Palm Sunday I was a part of a few years back now. I was serving as interim minister at a church in Columbia, Missouri—wonderful university town, and a wonderful church: beautiful sanctuary with beautiful liturgy, and splendid saints of God.

The church, that town really, has an annual tradition. On Palm Sunday the downtown churches gather for a procession of palms. The Presbyterians, Disciples, Methodists, Baptists, Lutherans, Catholics—they all gather. The service starts at 10:30, with some of the folks having just come from a worship service and some on their way back to one. The whole thing takes place on Broadway. That's the name of their main street through downtown. It's a typical main street in a college town—little sandwich shops, stores where you can buy University of Missouri shirts, music stores with all the latest CDs. It's the kind of street college kids might cruise down some Saturday night, or where Tiger fans might gather to celebrate the occasional, miraculous victory over Nebraska.

But this was a Sunday morning celebration of Palm Sunday, not a Saturday night football game. It was just some Christians waving palm branches in the streets while the city slept. Crowd control was not an issue. Kind of like this morning in Kansas City. I don't know about you, but I didn't have to make a detour to get here because of a bunch of rowdy Christians in the streets somewhere—not hardly.

So on a scale of 1 to 10, I'd say that Palm Sunday is about a 1. Yeah, about a 1. There's nothing all that triumphant about Jesus' entry into Jerusalem. In fact, the designation "triumphal entry" is not in the biblical text. Some editors in Nashville or Grand Rapids might call it that, but not Matthew. He doesn't call it anything; he just tells the story, and it doesn't really appear to be the kind of thing that would make *Headline News,* not even the little ticker tape across the bottom—not hardly. Along with thousands of pilgrims, a rabbi with a few followers enters Jerusalem at the time of Passover. Not exactly a big deal.

Oh, there were some "Hosannas" in the air, but most scholars believe that what originally was a cry for deliverance, "Save us now," had become in the time of Jesus sort of a half-hearted "Hurrah."[16] There are no palms in Matthew's version of the story. And as for his line about the "whole city" stirred up and the crowds proclaiming this and that, well…Matthew's a preacher. You've heard of the expression *ministerially speaking,* haven't you? Preachers tend to exaggerate. Not me, of course, or your pastor, Holly, but some preachers do. Matthew tries to make a big deal of it. He really does, but it's a small story.

Kansas City's Saint Patrick's Day parade—that's a big deal. I'd say it's about a 6 as such parades go. The ones in Chicago, New York, maybe a 7 or 8; and of course Dublin and Belfast would be 10s. Those are big ones. But this entry narrative in Matthew, it's not that big. On a scale of 1 to 10, about a 1. Hurrah.

You see, the people of Jerusalem knew triumphal entries. The ancient Mediterranean world was replete with triumphal entries—conquering armies with generals mounted on stallions, riding in to claim their spoils. And here comes Jesus, clip-clopping on a donkey with just a few disciples to claim as his own. It's sort of embarrassing really. Not very triumphant.

An Episcopal priest friend of mine was telling me recently about a time she was on a tour bus in Cairo: all these Americans with their fat wallets, cameras around their necks, bags full of souvenirs, sitting on this huge air-conditioned bus. They were sitting at a traffic light, when out the window she spied this large man riding atop a little donkey. She said the donkey was galloping, so that this poor figure was bouncing up and down, hardly able to keep his balance. "Trust me," she said, "it was not a triumphant entry." She said it was more comical than anything. Same thing here in Matthew's version. Not very triumphant.

Unless...unless you consider the value of street theater. That's what this is in a fashion—street theater. And as one New Testament scholar puts it, in this scene Jesus makes an ass out of Rome.[17] He does not enter as warrior, but a humble and gentle teacher. In satirical fashion he pokes fun at the military leaders of his day, the people of power.

But only for those who see, and the reason I say that is because of the way Matthew tells the story. Just prior to this, Matthew tells of the healing of two blind men, their eyes being opened. Then Jesus enters the city. It's Matthew's way of alerting us that this entry narrative is for those who truly see.

I think it was about a year ago this spring that one beautiful Saturday afternoon I had gone to the Home Depot near our house—maybe even last summer. We were adding to our landscape some of those bricks you line gardens with, build walls, that sort of thing. Well, we had decided to build the "Great Wall of China," and so I made multiple trips. I knew that the downtown airport was hosting an air show that same day, with some of the events involving military planes—you know, all those impressive jets screeching through the sky.

On one of my trips to Home Depot, they did a fly-over. I'm not really a plane buff, so you will probably pick up on my cynicism when I describe a fly-over as a chance to burn up some expensive fuel at taxpayer's expense, simply in order to impress the crowds—that sort of thing. Very triumphant. I was loading my bricks, when the rumble started. It's not the kind of thing you can ignore. Everyone stopped (okay, that's hyperbole), but several of us paused and looked. I tried to resist. It was hard not to look. They flew over and circled back to the airport. Then the woman who worked in the lawn and garden area said exactly what I had been thinking, only the way she said it was entirely different than the tone I would have used. She said, "Man, I'll bet that scares the hell out of those folks living in Baghdad." That's what she said.

I was numb. I may have muttered something, but I don't think I did. I don't know if she would have heard me over the rumble anyway. I have thought of so many things I wish I had said, things I have replayed in my mind. Just this week I thought of the story Anne Lamott tells, the one about jets flying over a playground in the States and the children who were suddenly scared. A teacher assured them the planes were not going to drop bombs on any of them. She said, "It's okay. They are going somewhere else." Then, wouldn't you know it, one of the kids asked, "Do they have children there who play outside?"[18]

This past week on spring break I took my daughter to visit Princeton, the place she dreams of attending when she graduates high school. We did the campus tour thing, asked a lot of questions, tried to figure out where our family would live if we sold the house to pay for tuition, that sort of thing. One night we went down to a coffee shop across from campus, Melissa typing out her college-bound thoughts on my laptop and me with Lamott's book and *The New York Times*. I read one passage from the book aloud to her, a story the rabbis tell about how if you live with God's word long enough you can put it on your heart. To which the disciples reply, "Why on our hearts and not in them?" The answer: "Because only God can put the Scriptures in your heart, but if you put it on your heart, then when your heart breaks the word will get inside."[19] Melissa smiled. I took a sip of my hot chocolate, then picked up *The Times*.

On the cover was the story of that judge, you know, Judge Joan Humphrey Lefkow, whose husband and mother were assassinated a few weeks ago. You saw that story, didn't you? I read the cover story, then flipped to page 22 to read the rest. It was the kind of story that kicks you in the stomach. Caring for her four daughters, trying to cope, hiding under police protection. Then, near the end, this one amazing line of how Judge Lefkow has found strength in a sermon she heard years ago at Saint Luke's Episcopal Church in Evanston, Illinois. The word was on her heart all those years, and then when her heart broke, God put it inside her. That's the entry of Jesus into Jerusalem—gentle.

And so, with the disciples of old, we lift up our Hosannas, gentle prayers for God to save us now. Come, Lord Jesus. Come into our cities. Come into Baghdad. Come into Kansas City. Come into our hearts. Save us now, we pray, save us even from ourselves. Amen.

CHAPTER 6

Matthew 25:14–30

Jesus Tells a Parable

Locating the Sermon

Twenty-sixth Sunday after Pentecost (Year A)

For weeks on end the gospel reading has come from Matthew, although not necessarily all our sermons. Even those who follow the Lectionary religiously do not always preach from the gospel text-segments. Regardless, with today's reading we near the end of our time in Matthew, with Year B only two weeks away, and a shift toward Mark.

Following this week's reading is the so-called parable of the sheep and goats on Christ the King Sunday. What a golden opportunity to contrast these two stories, as we shall see, highlighting the true nature of Christ's expectations for his followers.

Of course, approaching this text-segment, like the one last week—the parable of the bridesmaids—takes us back to a much earlier portion of Matthew's gospel, one we would have considered closer to Pentecost—namely, the parables in chapter 13. Therefore, as we consider the parable before us this week, we will need to look back briefly at that earlier chapter (13:1–17), reflecting on how parables function in general, and especially in Matthew.

As always, the kind of literature we are dealing with is significant. For many listeners the parables of Jesus are simple stories he told so that even kids could understand, when in reality they are more like riddles that more often than not confuse us and tease us. Even for some preachers, the parables of Jesus seem "preacher-friendly," as Thomas Long put it, only to discover they are some of the hardest passages to exegete and preach.[1] Therefore, as usual we will begin with a closer examination of the text-segment.

Understanding the Passage

While Jesus was known for his deeds of healing and exorcism, he is also portrayed in the gospels as an unparalleled wordsmith. Storytelling was an admired trait in the Mediterranean oral culture, and Jesus' parables demonstrated his ability to engage and challenge listeners. Matthew 25:14–30, the parable of the talents, is one of these engaging stories of comparison about the reign (*basileia*) of heaven. As N.T. Wright insightfully notes, the purpose of Jesus' story-parables was to break "open the worldview of Jesus' hearers, so that it could be remoulded [*sic*] into the worldview which he, Jesus, was commending. His stories, like all stories in principle, invited his hearers into a new world, making the implicit suggestion that the new worldview be tried on for size with a view of permanent purchase."[2]

When it comes to "trying on" this familiar parable, many preachers and listeners follow a traditional interpretive path that understands this parable as a call to be responsible with the gifts and skills that God has given to an individual. "If one does not use what one has been given, it will be taken away." The exegetical insights below, however, will challenge readers to see this parable from a very different angle. This parable calls for an interpreter to be extremely considerate of its social and cultural background, and also sensitive to its unique literary features. When an interpreter is considerate and sensitive, the traditional interpretation of this parable is challenged and a radically different worldview is presented for contemporary Christians.

How the Evangelist Crafted the Text-segment

Matthew 25:14–30 occurs within the context of the fifth and last discourse section in Matthew. This last discourse begins in 23:1 and finally ends with these words: "When Jesus had finished saying all these things…" (26:1a). As Matthew presents these last teachings of Jesus, he is quickly moving toward the time of Jesus' arrest, trial, and crucifixion. Therefore, these final words given during the time of impending crisis carry extra weight.

The parable of the talents is nestled between the parable of the ten bridesmaids (Mt. 25:1-13) and the Son of Man's judgment of the nations narrative in 25:31–46. Matthew has creatively connected together these three narratives. Each of these narratives is linked by the theme about someone who is coming and the response made to the final arrival of the "coming one." In the bridesmaids parable, it is a bridegroom; in the talents, it is a master; and in the judgment, it is the Son of Man. This eschatological theme certainly reflects a concern in Matthew's day regarding the perceived delayed *parousia* of Christ.[3] Collectively these parables emphasize the importance for Matthew's community to wait with continuing anticipation for the coming of Christ even in the face of lack of certainty about the timing of his return.

While the theme of returning is readily seen, the more one begins to explore these three parables individually, the more one realizes that their connection and arrangement are a creation of Matthew. The original *Sitz im Leben* (setting in life) for each individual narrative, while difficult to know for certain, can be a helpful approach to see more in the parable of the talents than has traditionally been noted. Stepping back and reflecting on the parable of the talents—less from the immediate context of Matthew's community and its eschatological concern, and more from the context of Jesus' original listeners and their immediate concerns—will provide additional perspectives for a preacher as he or she is preparing to proclaim this parable. We will explore these implications later in this chapter.

The parable of the talents is often evaluated in relationship to the parable of the pounds found in Luke 19:11–27. Points of similarities exist between these two parables, but there are also points of great difference. For example, while the elite portrayed in Matthew is a master (Mt. 25:19), in Luke's version it is a nobleman who is seeking royal power (Lk. 19:12). The number of servants and amounts given to them also varies greatly. The Lukan account has ten servants, although only three are called before the nobleman; and they are given ten pounds, which implies each received one pound (Lk. 19:13). Each pound (*mina*) would be equivalent to 100 drachmas (silver coins). The amounts are greatly increased in Matthew's version, and each servant is given differing amounts of talents. A talent is equivalent to 6000 drachmas (silver coins), and so the first servant received 30,000 silver coins; the second, 12,000 silver coins; and the last, 6000 silver coins.

The rewards given to the "profitable" servants are also quite different in the two versions. In Matthew they are told that they will be put "in charge of many things" (vv. 21, 23), but what those things are is left ambiguous. In the Lukan account, the servants are put specifically in charge of cities (vv. 17, 19). The textual contexts of the parables are quite different. Luke's version is given by Jesus just after his encounter with Zacchaeus (Lk. 19:1–10) and before Jesus enters Jerusalem (Lk. 19:28–48). In Matthew's version Jesus has already entered Jerusalem back in chapter 21. Matthew places his version of this parable in the context of two other parabolic stories as noted above.

Also, the Lukan and Matthean versions present slightly different phrases related to the reign (*basileia*) of God/Heaven. Luke indicates that Jesus tells this parable because the disciples supposed that the "kingdom of God was to appear immediately" (Lk. 19:11). Matthew rarely uses the phrase "kingdom of God" but instead uses, "Then the Kingdom of heaven will be like this" (25:1). While this phrase is not found in the parable of the talents, it is certainly implied in the introduction to the parable: "For it is as…" (25:14). The antecedent of "it" must be the reign (*basileia*) of heaven. Matthew's usage of heaven carries the same meaning as the reign (*basileia*) of God. It is a circumlocution readily understandable for the original Judean-Christian audience hearing this gospel.

All of these differences, and there are others, may lead an interpreter to even question whether these stories are actually parallel or not. At the very least, it should lead an interpreter to consider carefully what Matthew has done with this parable as opposed to the Lukan version of the parable, and to avoid harmonizing the accounts together.

Since Matthew 24:14–30 in form is a parable, one fruitful area for an interpreter to explore is the nature and characteristic of parables. Scholars and preachers have devised about as many definitions of parables as there are New Testament scholars and preachers. While the various definitions of a parable have points of similarity, several very different facets of parables are highlighted by different interpreters.[4] A classic definition, however, that seems to capture many of the most intriguing aspects of a parable comes from C.H. Dodd:

> At its simplest the parable is a metaphor or simile drawn from nature of common life, arresting the hearer by its vividness or strangeness, and leaving the mind in sufficient doubt about its precise application to tease it into active thought.[5]

Contained within this definition are all the categories a preacher needs for evaluating parables: (1) its metaphorical nature, (2) its origin within a specific historical/cultural context, (3) its strange twist, ambiguous nature, or surprising ending, and (4) its ability to put a reader into the story and cause him or her to think.

Perhaps one of the most delightful aspects of parables is also the most frustrating: they are full of ambiguity. Parables cannot, and should not, be reduced to one simple moralistic lesson. Yet interpreters often attempt to dissect and pin down "*the*" interpretation of a parable. When this happens, the parable either dies, or it slips away and one is left looking foolish while holding an empty story where a parable used to be. Perhaps one of the most appropriate ways to describe an approach to the parable of the talents, or any parable, is with a simple parabolic image: a kaleidoscope.

A kaleidoscope is a wonderfully simple device that fascinates both adults and children. It is a cylinder in which long glass mirrors are arranged at angles to each other. At the end of the cylinder are a few colored pieces of glass or plastic. When you hold a kaleidoscope up to the light, peer into the eyepiece, and twist it, color patterns appear. Even though the colored glass is the same and never changes in and of itself, with every twist of the kaleidoscope a new pattern emerges. The pattern of what you see depends on how you turn the kaleidoscope and from what angle you peer. So it is with a parable. How do we hold it and twist it within our mind's eye? Whether we approach a parable from its metaphor/simile perspective, from its social and cultural angle, from the strangeness contained within it, or from our own social location, it all depends on how we hold it and twist it. Especially when the parable of the talents is approached from the social and cultural angle, a new and challenging pattern is revealed in this story.

What the Text-segment Meant to the Community

One part of the definition that Dodd presented about parables is that they are "drawn from nature or common life." This statement seems self-evident, but contemporary preachers and interpreters must be careful in not imposing on the world of the parable the world of today: "When the full curtain on the common life of the ancient world is raised, it reveals a complex cultural and social stage on which all the parables are acted out. Yet the parable's common life element,…is often ignored or given only a superficial and cursory treatment in interpretation."[6] When a twenty-first–century worldview is imposed on the world revealed in and through parables, a distorted eisegesis of the parable takes place. This distortion is most evident in this parable of the talents.

The parable of the talents has most frequently been approached from an allegorical perspective. The talents, which as noted above are monetary units, are allegorized into the skills and gifts of individuals. The slaves are allegorized into contemporary Christians, and the master is God. In this typical interpretation, individuals are extolled to use, or risk, their gifts in the service of God. If one does not have adventuresome faith, then one can lose his or her gift. The problem with this interpretation is that it is anachronistic since the parable is read from contemporary social and cultural values.

One example of this anachronistic approach is the lack of understanding about the limited good society of first-century Mediterraneans. In their view of the world, all goods, tangible and intangible, existed in a finite limited amount. To be gaining more was always at the expense of someone else. Therefore in this parable, for the two "good" servants to get more for their master, then someone—most likely the original peasants gathered around hearing this parable—would have to be losing. Contemporary interpreters have lauded these two servants when they actually are henchmen doing the exploitive work of the master. As Richard Rohrbaugh, who has written most insightfully on this text-segment, succinctly says, "The 'venturesome' and 'industrious' pair [of servants] could be heroes only to those who believed it right to amass wealth by contriving to get a bigger share of the limited pie. The third servant, the one who gained nothing, could be viewed as 'wicked' only by persons with this same elitist mentality."[7]

Interpreters anachronistically portray the third servant not only as wicked but also as lazy. If he were being assessed from a capitalistic and twenty-first–century view (especially by a CEO of a corporation), perhaps this would be an accurate assessment. If someone is not a producer, based on our social values and work ethic, he or she is lazy. It is not surprising that preachers from many pulpits proclaim this third servant as bad and lazy since commentaries reinforce this servant as bad and lazy. A close and careful reading of this parable, however, highlights that the issue with the third servant is not laziness, but fear. In verse 25 he explicitly tells the master that he was afraid (*phobetheis*). The third servant was fearful in the face of doing the right action (preserving the master's money) while also not exploiting and taking money from someone else by trading, investing, or usury. In verse 26 the master castigates the servant by declaring him evil and *oknere*. Most translations use such words as *slothful* (RSV) or *lazy* (NRSV, NIV) for the Greek word *oknere*. However, this word translated as "lazy" more typically carries the meaning of fear.[8] It was the type of cringing fear often associated with slaves in relationship to masters.

To hear this parable, the way most original listeners would have, is to have sympathy and empathy for the last servant who does what is right and honorable—even in the face of certain retribution from the all-powerful master. Masters had the power of life and death over slaves. To go against the machination of the master was a fearful gamble. As William Herzog writes, "The whistle-blower is not a fool. He realizes that he will pay a price, but he has decided to accept the cost rather than continue to pursue his [the master's] exploitive path."[9] If this is true, then, as Herzog notes, "The hero of the parable is the third servant."[10]

If the third slave is the hero, the villain is the master. To characterize the master in the category of villain may cause some interpreters to shake their heads in bewilderment, because he has typically been portrayed as representing God. This parable is so frequently allegorized that it is difficult to shake people awake with a different view of this master. If we were to allegorize this master, however, he is not a portrait of God, but would be much more representative of a Simon Legree and a pre-conversion Ebenezer Scrooge all rolled into one. As readers of this parable, we often skip over the assessment of the master by the third slave, and yet slaves were good at assessing masters whom they saw up close and personal everyday. The servant describes the master as "a harsh man, reaping where you did not sow, and gathering where you did not scatter seed" (v. 24). Lest we discount his witness to the master's character—because he is only a slave—note that the master affirms that this assessment is exactly who he is (v. 26). One simple question needs to be asked of every interpreter of this passage: Is this the kind of God we worship and serve? This image is not one of God, but encapsulates the exploitive nature of the elites and powerful. Most of the peasants who originally heard this parable would more than likely "have nodded their heads in knowing agreement as Jesus pegged the unholy greed of the elite for what it was."[11]

The immediate context of this parable of the talents can both help and confuse an interpreter. The author has connected this parable with the parables of the ten maidens (25:1–13) and the faithful or unfaithful slave (24:45–51). There is little doubt that Matthew's redactional hand is evident with these parables. As noted earlier (p. 95), the author's redaction is guided by his eschatological outlook. The almost fifty years of Jesus' absence had caused the preacher Matthew to adapt Jesus' parables for a new congregational situation: the delayed *parousia,* return, of Jesus. Therefore, Matthew transforms Jesus' parables into ones of watchfulness, anticipation, and activity for the in between time. However, the parable of the judgment of the nations in 25:31–46 helps provide a window into the parable of the talents and its more original focus in Jesus' setting in life. It illustrates why the master and his two henchmen are negative characters while the third servant is put forward as a model.

The judgment of the nations in 25:31–46 is connected to the parable of the talents by a small Greek word that is omitted in English translations: *de. De* is a conjunction typically translated as "but." It is a weak adversarial conjunction, yet does indicate a shift and change.[12] If the *de* is taken into consideration, one could summarize these two stories as different sides of the same coin. The masters of the world will judge based on how much one has gained in monetary terms for them, *but in contrast* the

Son of Man will judge based on what one has done for others: feeding, clothing, and visiting (vv. 35–36).

Interpretive Summary

J. Ramsey Michaels posits a most fascinating way in which to consider the parables of Jesus: "Jesus' parables (or at least some of them) are a retelling of what he himself has heard, or seen, from God. They may be described as stories his Father told him, or images his Father showed him."[13] These revelatory parables were ones Jesus would have first interpreted in the context of his own ministry. They would have been powerful moments for shaping his own self-identity and self-understanding.[14]

If this approach is sound, then this parable of the talents is even more fascinating for an interpreter, because it is possible that Jesus would have understood himself in the role of that third servant. Did Jesus see that the path he was taking was one that would ultimately end in his own death/exile, similar to that of the third servant?[15] Jesus is presented in Matthew's gospel as one who had already stood against exploitative monetary policies regarding temple practices (21:12–13). He is getting ready to be labeled by the powerful elites as blasphemous (26:65). They certainly would have viewed Jesus as anything but honorable. The passion narrative culminates with Jesus being cast out into the "outer darkness" of Golgotha. Perhaps this parable was a powerful revelatory experience for Jesus. If so, then it was a painful visionary foreshadowing for what would become the drama of Jesus' passion when a good and faithful slave/servant is mislabeled and cast out.

Preaching the Passage

The Familiar and Unfamiliar

We have repeatedly considered the distance between ourselves and ancient texts. Perhaps nowhere is this distance more pronounced than with the deceptively familiar parables of Jesus. Granted, we moderns recognize that farmers scattering seed by hand (13:1–9) and masters giving money to servants followed by an accounting of their stewardship (25:14–30) are dated images. We know that the Bible is set in a different time and place than ours, but these stories seem closer to us, more inviting. In these stories that Jesus spins, we enter a narrative world of the everyday, even if that day is two millennia removed.

As we shall see, this remains one of the biggest problems with parables, however—assuming too much familiarity. As we have already noted, C.H. Dodd's classic definition of a parable still stands the test of time, both from an interpretive standpoint but also a homiletical one.

Several aspects of his definition are worth noting, each with implications for how to preach parables that *do* what the parables of Jesus did over and over in their telling. In the previous section we noted how the "common life" from which the parables are drawn was a life common to first-century listeners, not twenty-first–century ones. Still, on the surface the parables seem quite accessible. Unlike our reading of Levitical codes in the Hebrew Scriptures, or even New Testament accounts about Pharisees and Sadducees, most of us can relate to stories about women baking bread (13:33), finding buried treasure (13:44), or, in this case, a master and his servants. But as Dodd wisely adds, these common life stories arrested Jesus' listeners by means of their "vividness or strangeness."

In other words, these riddle-like stories of Jesus are deceptively simple, deceptively familiar. One of the tasks as preachers today will be to overcome the cultural distance between our time and the ancients, only then to create another kind of distance created by the parable's twists. Or, to put it more succinctly, we may need to go along playfully with the traditional understanding of a story about using our "talents for God," before rhetorically switching to an alternative reading, one that challenges capitalism as the way for Christ's followers as opposed to caring for the hungry and homeless.

Making Connections

If we dare to preach this more radical reading of Jesus—an indictment against amassing wealth to the neglect of the poor—how then shall we go about the task? What does it mean for the preacher whose salary is paid by church members to challenge listeners with regards to monetary matters? How shall we, who are part of a system that gets ahead in this world on the backs of the poor, point our fingers against such injustice, even if the old saw reminds us that a pointed finger means three pointing back at us? We buy our produce at rock-bottom prices year-round, ignoring the toll this exacts on the migrant farm worker. How, then, shall we bear witness?

Perhaps the answer lies in the last question above, *bearing witness*. If we understand preaching not so much in terms of persuading others to some course of action ("How are you a part of the systemic injustice in our global economy? How might you live differently in light of this parable?"), but bearing witness, testifying to what is true and false in the world, then maybe the tenor of our preaching will be different.[16] Maybe part of that testimony will be corporate ("How are *we* a part of the systemic injustice in our global economy? How might *we* live differently in light of this parable?"), or perhaps personal ("So I ask myself, *How do I contribute to a system that exploits others when God's desire is not amassing more but feeding the poor?*").

When used wisely, testimony is a powerful asset in preaching.[17] Some of the most authentic preaching I have ever heard has wrestled with the preacher's own systemic involvement in fiscal injustice. Some of the most shallow preaching I have ever heard pretended to wrestle with the same matters. Listeners are quite efficient at judging the difference. Ultimately, our rhetoric will be judged on the basis of our actions—the church's, that is. If the minister continues to talk about justice issues on occasions like this but never proposes any changes in what it means to be church to the poor and to budget accordingly, then our words, to quote another well-known preacher in the New Testament, become like a noisy gong (1 Cor. 13).

Of course, any discussion of preaching from the parables must account for their open-ended quality and the tendency of our preaching to be anything but open-ended. The DNA of most of us preachers compels us to be clear and forthright, to "nail it down," as the old saying goes. While that approach would seem the only obvious one to take, it helps to recall that the parables of Jesus do not nail down much of anything. Richard Jensen, a homiletician who values the power of stories to do their work, parable or otherwise, suggests our sermon on this passage "will not need any explanations. No points need to be made. Let the stories do their work!" He adds, "If this open-endedness is too risky for you or your people, it might be well to close with a prayer that helps people gather up the stories for their own lives."[18]

Parables Then and Now: Stories for Sermons

Throughout our study of Matthew's gospel, we have noted the narrative quality of the text-segments before us—Jesus' parents fleeing with the toddler, his sitting on a mount as he pronounces a state of blessedness, walking (on water) out to a boat in the midst of a storm. These are stories about Jesus. In this segment of the gospel, we not only have the evangelist's story of Jesus but the interior story that Jesus tells, the parable itself.

Both are worthy of our attention in retelling during the sermon. It will be important for listeners to be reminded that Jesus now teaches for the last time, that he has come to the end of his earthly ministry and is casting an eye toward the future. It will also be important for listeners to hear the parable retold with a degree of imagination and engagement. Instead of simply *talking about* the parable, we must always keep in mind the importance of parables as stories. Therefore, we must *talk about* it as well as *tell* it.

Richard Jensen suggests that we might do well to retell not only the parable before us (the talents), but the cluster of three parables in this portion of Matthew: 24:45–51; 25:1–13; and 25:14–30, all of which have lords who assign tasks and, on returning, will expect an accounting. Although the interpretation we are suggesting might not work with that approach, given the contrast between the talents parable and the next one, we might think about combining a retelling of this week's text-segment with 25:31–46, depending on our focus for next week's sermon.

As for contemporary stories, we may need to consider all three of Thomas Long's helpful categories of illustration: analogy, example, and metaphor.[19] Analogies help us to understand concepts. For instance, in the sample sermon included here, the story is told of discovery at a museum, about the "Nora Fragment." The analogy functions to help listeners appreciate the upside-down nature of the parable of the talents.

Since example stories help listeners to experience what we are preaching about, stories of economic injustice would always be appropriate. Timeliness may be the key here. Listening to National Public Radio or reading the newspaper so as to include contemporary examples will be helpful. Sermons whose examples are dated will lessen the rhetorical impact. While fortunate for our purposes, the world is unfortunately full of daily examples of economic injustice.

Analogies and examples are the norm in our sermons, the week-to-week fare on which we rely as preachers. But Long's third category—metaphor—is especially appealing when the text-segment is a parable, since metaphor, as he notes, is "the instrument of poets." Metaphor is "the rarest type of illustration, and in some ways riskiest, because it sacrifices precision and clarity for the sake of imagination and multiple meanings."[20] What might it mean, for example, to tell a story that does not provide an example of injustice but only wrestles with the complexities of life and leaves things unsettled?

Sermon Possibilities

While the possibilities are not endless, there are possible options for preachers to weigh:
- Using Our Financial Resources for God
- Resisting the Ways of the Empire's Economics

Sample Sermon: Parable of the Talents

David May first preached this sermon on April 17, 1991, as a chapel address at Midwestern Baptist Theological Seminary. Its challenge to a traditional interpretation of the "parable of the talents" caused quite a stir among some of the seminary's board members. It is offered here as an example of parabolic preaching.

"When Good Is Bad...and Bad Is Good" ──────
A Sermon by David M. May

In the Mediterranean Sea, on the island of Sardinia, is a museum that contains a stone fragment on which are scrawled a few ancient letters. This venerated object is called the Nora Fragment and is believed to be the oldest example of a written script in existence. The fragment, which has been displayed for years, is admired by the public and studied by scholars. Recently, however, a scholar who was attempting to decipher the inscription jotted a note to the museum curator that said, "I don't want to be the one to embarrass anyone, but this fragment is displayed upside-down."[21] For all the years it was displayed, the admiring public accepted the fragment as correct, and scholars had even attempted to interpret its enigmatic scrawl. Yet it was upside down.

Parables are in some sense fragments; they are just small parts of Jesus' teachings. They have been admired and studied, but my suspicion is that on some occasions they need to be turned upside-down. So despite years of preaching and teaching on Matthew 25:14–30, what we call the parable of the talents,[22] I want to take it and turn it upside-down and in the process maybe we will all see it or hear it right-side up.

Most of us are very familiar with the typical teaching and preaching on this parable. These talents, which were first-century monetary units, are spiritualized as gifts that the master, that is, God, gives to all of us. This parable is proclaimed, therefore, as a warning to all those individuals who are not adventuresome in risking their faith and who are not industrious enough with their gifts. Usually preachers as they close their sermon on this passage will say, "You need to use what you've got or you will lose it," or, "Make an investment for God; risk it all for God."

This is *an* interpretation that has become *the* interpretation. It is the popular interpretation for both the pew and pulpit because of the economic presuppositions that both have. We have been born and educated into a system of economics that rewards those who invest and gain. This parable is at the very heart of the Protestant work ethic. Our heroes and heroines today are those who make money and are good at it. We usually look down on someone who is not a good businessman or woman. Lest you think that I am only talking about something that infects the Wall Street crowd who deal with millions, I also am talking about the Wal-Mart gang who hustle daily through its doors. It's the feeling one gets by saving $1.50 because it's double coupon day, *and* you have a rebate certificate of 50 cents, *and* the item is marked down because it's last year's model.

We assume the first listeners of this parable were like us and had our concerns about money and gaining and saving. We assume they were involved in a capitalist system like ours. Nothing could be further from the truth.

The original individuals who gathered around Jesus and heard this parable were peasants. This group had little to call its own and lived on only enough to survive from day to day. This lifestyle was not bad; it was just the way life was meant to be lived. The peasants assumed in their Mediterranean world of the first century that everything existed only in limited quantity. There was only so much of anything to go around. If you gain and accumulate money or wealth, if you become a capitalist, you are doing it at the expense of someone else. This accumulation, in their view, was wrong.

Consider also this perplexing question related to the ones making money in this parable: Where else in the gospels does Jesus commend getting wealthy at the expense of others? Rather, constantly on the lips of Jesus are those hard sayings that we choose to ignore or soften. In the story of the rich man and Lazarus, the rich man goes to Hades, and Lazarus to the bosom of Abraham. On another occasion, Jesus says to a rich young man, "Give *all* that you have and then, and only then, can you truly obtain the kingdom of God." Then Jesus tells his disciples it is easier for a camel to go through the eye of a needle than for a rich person to get into heaven.

In this parable, does Jesus reverse himself? Does he commend getting wealthy at the expense of others? If we turn this parable upside-down, perhaps our own outlook sees something new. Perhaps the focus falls not on the two servants whom we have always labeled as "good and trustworthy," and in the passage are commended, but it actually falls on the last servant. It's the last servant that we are to imitate!

Jesus often told parables and narratives in which the last element in the story is the one he commends. In the story of the soils and seeds, it is the last, rich soil that produces abundance, which is commended. In the parable of the Levite, priest, and Samaritan, it is the least likely and yet the last person we are pointed toward as our model. I invite you to consider in the parable of the talents that we are to place ourselves in the role of the *last* servant, who is a positive model for us, and not with the two who have been labeled as good and usually cited as our model.

Ask yourselves, Are those two servants really "good"? These servants are henchmen of the master. They throw in their lot with him. They go along with his schemes, and share his attitudes and philosophy. In the final assessment, they also share in his guilt of exploitation.

There are always those who attempt to make their lives easier by throwing in their lots with those who have the power.

While in Germany in 1976, I visited one of the few German concentration camps that have been preserved as memorials. It is called Dachau. During my visit, I saw the showers in which the Jews were herded and then gassed. I saw the ovens in which the bodies were then taken and cremated. Then I went to a building that housed numerous photographs taken during the concentration days of Dachau. Many of the photographs were enlarged so that the public could not miss the conditions that existed in this camp. In some of the pictures the faces of the Nazi guards had been scratched out. It was evident that someone had leaned over the handrail and out of anger mixed with anguish taken a pen or sharp instrument and defaced the face. However, I also noticed that once in a while a Jewish inmate in prison garb also had his face scratched out. I asked a guide why, and in scornful reply he stated, "Collaborators."

Collaborators, henchmen—those who go along to get along. Are we vulnerable at this level? Is lurking inside each of us the potential to be a collaborator with power? Could we or would we trade our integrity and honor for the price of a paycheck, a trip, an easier situation, a higher position—our lives? The first two servants, who are mistakenly labeled as "good," could see who held the strings of power and privilege, and, with unbounded energy, they went along with the master.

In contrast, the third servant did not go along. Instead, he did what was in Jewish tradition the most honorable action to follow. He took the talent given to him and buried it. This was the correct behavior. In his role, he was to care for, not endanger, what he had been entrusted. He was to be a steward, not an entrepreneur. The third servant does what is honorable, even in the face of great fear. Verse 24 records these words, and these are not words uttered in grandiose confidence but most likely with a hitch in the voice, downcast eyes, and quaking knees: "Master, I knew you were a harsh man, reaping where you did not sow, and gathering where you did not scatter seed." Is this a portrait of God? Is this the God we gather each Sunday to worship? No. However, it is a word picture in vivid colors of the world. It's a picture of power that demands and exploits those who cannot resist. The honorable servant finishes his speech before the all-powerful master by saying, "I knew you were a harsh man...[and I know that my fate is now inevitable so] here you have what is yours."

I discovered in my prowling through an old book store a beautiful first edition book by Karl Barth called *Credo*. It's a series of lectures he delivered in 1935 that were immediately translated into English in 1936. As I thumbed through the book, I turned to the dedication page and read these words:

1935!

TO THE MINISTERS

HANS ASMUSSEN, HERMANN HESSE, KARL IMMER,

MARTIN NIEMOLLER, HEINRICH VOGEL

In memory of all who

stood

stand

and will stand

In every age, generation, state, church, and denomination, calls come to face the masters. It is a call to stand against those individuals or groups who have the power to torment or even kill the flesh, but not the Spirit. It is in the face of that power to crush that we are evaluated as women and men of honor and integrity.

What does it mean to follow the honorable course? It may mean being labeled. Verse 30 indicates the third servant is labeled as "wicked and lazy." And so the labels have stuck as they have come down through the history of preaching. Somewhere this morning someone is castigating and vilifying that last poor servant. And perhaps we are all too ready without questioning to join others and label him, then dismiss him as useless. And when the label begins to stick, it is okay to see him as less than human—as someone who gets what he deserves.

Will the temporary pain of labels cause us to abandon the honor and Christlike way of life? The powerful masters are out there, and they demand that servants do their bidding, to follow a course of action that may have very little to do with being Christian. To be honorable means to maintain integrity and continue in the *followship* of Christ. It will be difficult and painful because the masters have all the worldly power at their disposal.

When you stand as an honorable servant before the powerful masters and say, "I will not follow. I will not do what you ask. I will be honorable in Christlike action," you may be ostracized. You may be labeled. You may even lose your position.

I know that I am speaking this morning to the cream of the crop when it comes to honor and integrity. You are the honorable people of God, and you are seeking to do God's ministry. This message this morning, therefore, may not seem like good news. It may seem like just the opposite—bad news. However, it is Jesus' way of saying to the audience then and saying to us gathered here today, "Be realistic. When you follow me, when you stand against power, when you speak the truth, be prepared for the consequences."

As Jesus points out in this parable, the reward may be to be cast out into darkness where "there will be weeping and gnashing of teeth." But remember, we are never truly alone in the darkness. Nor are we the first to tread the path called honor. Jesus, an honorable servant who was labeled as wicked, was cast into "the darkness" of Golgotha, where there was the weeping of women and the gnashing of teeth of those on either side of him. Yet, he was not truly alone; God was with him. In the immediacy of our separation and exile, we may indeed cry out as Jesus did, "God, why have you forsaken me?" But wait, actively endure, because the hope of the Christian faith is the resurrection.

For everyone here who stood, stands, and will stand against the powerful—against exploiters, the power seekers, the power users—and for those of us who simply hang on long enough to do what is honorable, we will be vindicated by God. Amen.

CHAPTER 7

Matthew 28:1–10

Jesus Raised from the Dead

Locating the Sermon

Easter Sunday (Year A)

If ever there were a passage easy to locate, this is it. The climactic Sunday of the Christian year has arrived. The "Alleluias" absent during Lent are now rolled out in hymns and litanies. Our explorations in Matthew that began with Mary and Joseph and the infant Jesus now bring us to his resurrection from the dead. As Dale Allison notes, chapter 28 is "the necessary ending to Matthew's story."[1] But while the resurrection (and later commissioning) are the end to Matthew's story, they are in many ways the beginning of the church's story.

Still, as central as resurrection is to the church's faith and very existence, it is ironically one of the harder passages to preach. Is there anything to say that has not been said before? Is repeating the grand story enough? Are apologetics in order? With what shall we help people to comprehend resurrection from the dead? What does Jesus' resurrection mean for us who are still alive? Preachers know stories about innocents slaughtered, temptation, those who hunger for righteousness, and oppressive economics; but how many of us have resurrection stories to tell? Or, as Thomas Long rightly notes, we modern preachers find ourselves straddling a huge precipice. On the historical side there is "a record of capital punishment and a few scraps of information about the beginnings of a religious movement," and on the other side the testimony of Peter and his colleagues transformed from cowards to martyrs.[2] What shall we say to that? As has been our custom throughout, we begin by seeking to understand the passage.

Understanding the Passage

The resurrection narrative in Matthew 28:1–10 is a familiar story and yet strangely fresh when read closely. An interpreter will do well to read Matthew's account carefully and on its own without harmonizing with the other gospels.[3] As no two snowflakes are alike, at least in folklore, so also the four resurrection narratives each offer their own unique perspective on what took place on the third day in an obscure tomb on the outskirts of Jerusalem. As an interpreter approaches Matthew's account, the other gospel narratives read in parallel (not harmony) will bring into stark relief Matthew's particular presentation of God's climatic and eschatological action of raising Jesus from the dead.

A perceptive reader of Matthew's resurrection account is also rewarded by reading it within the context of the entire gospel. By holding in one's mind previous themes, scenes, and sayings, an interpreter will sense the author's careful attention to both literary composition and theological persuasion. The author of Matthew was seeking to articulate for his original listeners a new approach to ethics, community, mission, and relationship with God. For Matthew, this new worldview found both its foundation stone and capstone in the resurrection of Jesus of Nazareth.

How the Evangelist Crafted the Text-segment

What might be surprising to an interpreter is the relatively brief account of Jesus' resurrection. While the entire gospel of

Matthew prepares a listener for this event, the story of Jesus' resurrection is recounted in only ten verses. The immediate context, however, helps give the account shape and definition, and it also helps illustrate the resurrection as the climatic ending for the gospel. As so often seems in Matthew's compositional style, a chiastic structure can be discerned in 27:57—28:20. The resurrection narrative (28:1–10) serves as the nodal point around which the ending of Matthew revolves. Its immediate context is the story of the guards in 27:62–66 and 28:11–15. The resurrection and guard stories in turn are bracketed by Jesus' burial, which creates the sense that death has taken his presence away for good (27:57–61), and by the great commission, in which readers learn the truth that Jesus is present always (28:16–20). The following outline illustrates the flow of Matthew's composition.

27:57–61 The Burial of Jesus and His Absence
27:62–66 Guard Story
28:1–10 Resurrection Story
28:11–15 Guard Story
28:16–20 The Commission by Jesus and His Presence

The burial of Jesus introduces Joseph of Arimathea, Mary Magdalene, and the other Mary. These quiet disciples, under the watchful eye of authorities, demonstrated the staying power of loyalty even unto death. The eleven disciples, strangely, are not there, or perhaps it is not so strange. The Eleven have demonstrated once again they are fearful and "men of little faith" (8:26; 14:31; 16:8). While it could be easy to condemn their fleeing and fleeting discipleship, the counterpart to this scene in 28:16–20 illustrates they are reconciled to Jesus by receiving his commission of the gospel message. Matthew highlights that, on both sides of the resurrection, forms of discipleship exist. Who is to say what discipleship action is most important, and who is to say at what point one's discipleship might fail? Matthew has prepared listeners so that they might identify with any or all the disciples who surround the resurrection.

The guard stories of 27:62–66 and 28:11–15 form the immediate context around the resurrection account and are unique to Matthew. They function as an apologetic since the author makes it clear that in his day (28:15) many did not believe Jesus had been raised from the dead. As W.D. Davies and Dale Allison note, "Evidently the Jewish opponents of Matthean Christianity...did not dispute the historicity of the empty tomb but rather assigned its cause to the theft in the cause of piety."[4] Therefore, the rumor circulating among the Judeans was that Jesus' body had been stolen by his disciples (28:13). The inclusion of the guard stories served to defend against such allegations.

The request for guards to secure the tomb originates with the chief priests and the Pharisees (27:62). The author illustrates that just as the Pharisees plagued Jesus in life, they do so also in death. In Matthew's characterization, especially the Pharisees continually oppose Jesus. Anthony Saldarini succinctly summarizes the author's situation, "Matthew is engaged in lively and serious controversy with his fellow late 1st-century Jews."[5] Through the guard stories, Matthew portrays the leadership of the Judean community in the worst possible light. They are paranoid and cover-up specialists who resort to bribes. As Saldarini notes, "The author of Matthew seeks specifically to delegitimate the traditional, established leadership of the Jewish community and thus legitimate his own group and its authority."[6]

It is a helpful reminder that Matthew's gospel is, in part, an example of intra-Judean conflict and polemics. Allegations and charges were being lobbed back and forth between Judean leadership and Matthew's group. Their battles, however, are not the battles of modern listeners. When culturally specific Judean polemics of the first century are interpreted to highlight the superiority of Christianity, they operate as anti-Semitic interpretations. Interpreters would be well served to be sensitive to the caricature of Judeans in passages such as the guard stories.[7]

The guard stories, along with the previous crucifixion scene, recall for an interpreter the continuing presence of Empire. The guard of soldiers is usually understood as being Roman, since the Judean leaders asked permission from Rome's power broker Pilate.[8] At the beginning of Matthew's gospel, Jesus' life is threatened when the Roman client-king Herod dispatches henchmen to execute all the male children in Bethlehem two years or younger (2:16–18). The Empire wreaks violence in its wake at both the beginning and ending of Jesus' life. If at the beginning of Jesus' life some sought to silence any messianic hopes by slaughter, those at the end hoped to silence any rumor about resurrection by bribery. The author illustrates that every strategy employed by the Empire fails.

The writer of Matthew locates the resurrection encounter as "After the sabbath, as the first day of the week was dawning" (v. 1a). The precision of this statement is grounded in what had become by the author's time a sacred time, Sunday. The "first day of the week" was a time to affirm anew that the tomb was empty and that Jesus had indeed risen. For the original listeners, each Sunday gathering was a miniature resurrection experience (Acts 20:7; 1 Cor. 16:2). It was not just a yearly event but a weekly encounter with the risen Christ.

Mary Magdalene and the other Mary are described as going to see the tomb. When the resurrection accounts of the gospels are compared, a great deal of variety is found regarding who was going to the tomb and for what purpose. One constant, however, is Mary Magdalene.[9] While the other Mary's identity remains ambiguous, it nevertheless calls the reader's attention back to the beginning of the gospel to "another" Mary who was the mother of Jesus (1:18–24). Women named Mary bracket the life of Jesus and demonstrate righteousness and piety in their actions.

Another major difference in Matthew's account is the reason for going to the tomb. In the Markan and Lukan accounts, the women go to anoint with spices (Mk. 16:1; Lk. 24:1). Matthew, however, has the women going to the tomb simply to see.

Yet is seeing ever that simple in Matthew? Seeing is one of those Matthean themes that sneaks under the radar because it is so simple and taken for granted. Warren Carter, however, notes, "Verbs of seeing have been especially important in the gospel. Having 'eyes to see' or 'seeing' are metaphors that denote understanding (9:2) or insight into Jesus' teaching, and experience of that reality to which it testifies (13:16-17; cf. 5:8)."[10] A sensitive reader of 28:1–10 will highlight the frequent usage of seeing: verses 1, 6, 7, 10.

The act of seeing distinguishes true disciples. One is reminded of the powerful story that ripples forward from chapter 25. The righteous ones see the hungry, thirsty, stranger, sick, naked, and prisoner (25:34–40). This type of seeing provokes incarnational actions of discipleship toward those in need of mercy and compassion.

Verse 2 signals for the interpreter that the women have encountered an eschatological moment. The eschatological characteristic of this moment is evident first by an earthquake— the world is shifting.[11] It is not shifting just or only physically, but also spiritually. This spiritual dimension is revealed by the detailed angelophany.

The angel is introduced as descending from heaven, a typical detail in the Judean apocalyptic tradition, and as having the appearance of lightning. The text-segment also presents the angel as having strength enough to remove the stone from the entrance of the tomb and to sit royally upon it. The angel is specifically referenced as an angel of the Lord. This is not the first time an angel of the Lord makes an appearance in the gospel of Matthew. The angel of the Lord appeared at the beginning of the gospel at a critical moment in Joseph's decision-making (1:20). Just as the angel gave Joseph instructions to follow about Jesus' name and, more importantly, Jesus' role, so the angel in this resurrection account gives instructions that are righteously obeyed.

Unlike the figurine angels often hawked today, the Hebrew Scriptures presented the agents of God as powerful figures who were overwhelmingly terrifying. The fearful reaction of the guards is typical of angelophanic encounters found in the Hebrew tradition. The author, however, splashes in a touch of irony in the reaction of the guards to their angelophany. The guards, who were meant to guard the dead, become themselves "like dead men" (v. 4). The one who was dead, however, is very much alive.

While all interpreters are familiar with the great commission (28:16–20), often the "*first* commission" in 28:5–8 gets overlooked. Perhaps its neglect is due to its being delivered by an angel and not by Jesus and being given to women and not to "the" Eleven. This commission, however, represents the first acknowledgment about Jesus' transformed status and is the heart of the resurrection message.

Several aspects of this first commission to the women stand out in dramatic relief in this text-segment. First is the interesting identification of Jesus "who was crucified" (v. 5). An original listener or reader who knew the story well might have expected the angel to say, "I know that you seek Jesus the raised one," or, "Jesus the resurrected one." Instead, it is Jesus' continuing identity as crucified that is highlighted. It is highlighted even more in the Greek.

The form for "crucified" is a perfect participle. Joseph Webb and Robert Kysar note, "When the perfect tense appears in a text, it is always a significant occurrence... This is a powerful Greek tense, and often very telling and distinctive, particularly in the theological language of the New Testament."[12] In essence, the perfect participle implies that Jesus is "the one who has been crucified and continues to exist as crucified." Eugene Boring puts it succinctly, "Even as the risen one, he bears the mark of his self-giving on the cross as his permanent character and call to discipleship."[13] Resurrection does not mean the erasure of the past, but rather the transformation of the past for living in the present. This image is vividly captured and portrayed by John the author of the Apocalypse when he writes that he saw "a Lamb standing as if it had been slaughtered" (Rev. 5:6). When kingdoms conflict, the stigmata of violence does not vanish but remains as a reminder or badge. Paul, an early proclaimer of the risen Christ, notes this truth well in his own ministry (Gal. 6:17).

The angel announces a fact to the women regarding the tomb, "He is not here," and then provides an explanation, "for he has been raised" (v. 6).[14] Significantly, this announcement is given in a form often called the "divine passive." Jesus did not raise himself from the grave, but was raised by God. The core theological truth of the New Testament and the Hebrew Scriptures is that God is the author of life, and God knows no experience of death. It is God who gifts life. Unlike the Greek concept that posits immortality of the soul as an innate part of human nature, the Christian perspective affirms that life as represented by resurrection originates and is given only by God.

The women are given a specific commission. They are instructed to tell Jesus' disciples that (1) he has been raised, and (2) that Jesus will meet them in Galilee where they will see him for themselves (v. 7). This entrusted message for the women places them as the first gospelers, the apostles to the apostles. As Boring also notes, "The women become not only missionaries of the resurrection, but also agents of reconciliation."[15] The Eleven did not leave Jesus under the best of circumstances; they fled, denied, and betrayed. The women are given the task of announcing to the disciples (whom Jesus calls brothers in v. 10) that they are still part of the family. In the gospel of Matthew the reconciliation between community members is a recurring theme (ch. 18). By the message the women carry to the Eleven, they illustrate that Jesus is not only the resurrected one but also the forgiving and reconciling one.

The contrast between the actions of the women in Matthew and Mark is significant. In the Markan account, after the women are commissioned, the author writes that they fled from the tomb and, "said nothing to anyone, for they were afraid" (Mk. 16:8). In Matthew's account the women also experience fear

(28:8). The difference, however, is that the fear is tempered by "great joy." The women, like many characters in Matthew's gospel, put divine instructions into immediate action as they seek to fulfill the commission.

Unexpectedly for the women, and interpreters, they encounter the risen Jesus on the way to fulfill their angelic commission. What is also surprising is the casual greeting Jesus gives to the women. While the NRSV translates this initial salutation as "Greetings!" the contemporary equivalent is "Good morning" (v. 9). Clarence Jordan in his *Cotton Patch* translation perhaps best captures the casual greeting with the phrase, "Howdy."[16] The simplicity of the greeting, however, belies the significance of the encounter. An interpreter is reminded of the eschatological import by Jesus' command to the women not to fear, the same command the angel gave earlier.

The women react to this encounter with Jesus by grasping his feet and worshiping (28:9). This scene continues the Matthean emphasis upon worship and will be repeated in the reaction of the Eleven when they meet Jesus (28:17). Matthew has framed his gospel with the bookends of worship. The gospel began with stargazers from the East who worshiped Jesus at his birth (2:2, 11), and it ends with amazed women and dazed disciples worshiping Jesus at his rebirth. This worship focus is a reminder for interpreters that the core identity for the early Israelites revolved around the worship of God. This same core identity is continued in the lives of Jesus' followers. What becomes unique, however, is that the focus of worship centers on Jesus.

After Jesus' initial greeting and the command against fear, he issues a second commissioning. This second commission is perplexing because its inclusion is unnecessary. The women are on the way to deliver the message entrusted by the angel, and the commission Jesus gives them in 28:10 is virtually identical to the angel's. Why a second commission? To double a message or incident is to put an explanation point to it. In essence the women are commissioned to begin telling the story of Jesus being raised and alive. This commission, however, is a radically new story that the author wants the readers or listeners to savor and inwardly digest; it has far-reaching implications. It is not just the exciting news that Jesus is back; this type of news is the kind many individuals have experienced in learning that an ill friend or family member has gotten better. Rather, this story is a *new* story that death "is not something which has to structure every human life from within...but rather it is an empty shell, a bark without a bite."[17] Jesus, Paul, John the Seer, the writer of Hebrews (Priscilla?) and countless others have understood that death is not the beating drum by which we march, but it is the God-giftedness-of-life, resurrection, that guides us, informs us, and gives us meaning.

What the Text-segment Meant to the Community

Resurrection stands at the center of the Christian kerygma. In the great liturgical affirmation, "Christ has died, Christ is risen, Christ will come again," resurrection bridges the past and future. John Jansen's words provide an appropriate reflection and conclusion on the resurrection:

> New Testament faith confesses that in a particular past, the history of Jesus of Nazareth, God has acted decisively by raising him from the dead. That past ensures the future and governs the present. Because Easter has its own time and place it can touch every time and every place.[18]

Preaching the Passage

The Familiar and Unfamiliar

More than once we have noted the distance between ourselves and text-segments, but nowhere is this distance more pronounced than with the resurrection of Jesus from the dead. All of us have known people who died; we know no one who has been raised from the dead. We greet one another on Easter morning with the traditional exchange: "Christ is risen." "He is risen indeed." Still, we're not sure what to make of that information. If we leave it at just that, as information, then what we have is the following threadbare plot in Matthew's telling:

> Early on Sunday morning two women visit the tomb where Jesus has been buried.
> The earth quakes.
> An angel who has rolled back the stone sits atop it.
> The Roman guards shake with fear, while the angel tells the women not to be afraid.
> The one for whom they look has been raised from the dead.
> They are to tell this to the disciples.
> Going, Jesus greets them and tells them not to be afraid.
> They are to tell this to the others who will see him.

Clearly, the exegetical considerations we have examined point to a much more complex reading than this. But what is the significance for Sunday's sermon?

As we noted in chapter 14, miracle stories are not so much about the miracle as the story that gets told through that miracle. This holds true with the resurrection of Jesus, even if the stakes seem higher from a historical point of view. As Donald Hagner rightly notes, "The narrative presupposes the resurrection of Jesus rather than giving an account of how or when it happened." He adds that the text-segment is "fundamentally an announcement" of the resurrection.[19] Apologetic approaches to the resurrection often discount the meaning of the story in favor of defending the historicity of the event, usually in an attempt to convince unbelievers. Scores of books continue to take such an approach, often using courtroom metaphors—Lee Strobel's *The Case for Christ: A Journalist's Personal Investigation of the Evidence for Jesus,* for example.[20]

The evangelist, however, addresses a community of *believers,* and not with courtroom testimony but *story.*[21] The story elements of the resurrection are loaded with meaning: darkness giving way to light, Rome's soldiers becoming like dead men, encouragement not to be afraid, Jesus raised from the dead, good news delivered by marginalized women, and restoration to the community for those disciples who earlier abandoned Jesus. The question is, How shall we communicate that meaning?

Making Connections

Even if we decide against an apologetic defense in favor of a narrative approach, certain elements of the text-segment still call for explanation. Deciding between *explanation* and *narration* need never be viewed as mutually exclusive. The preacher should note Warren Carter's observation about the prominence of *seeing* in this story.[22] Such a note need not be elaborate and labyrinthine. We are *preaching*, after all, not writing for the academy. For instance, the preacher might say something like this:

> Did you notice what Matthew wants us to *see*? This story emphasizes *seeing*. The women who, in chapter 27, *see* Jesus crucified, now go to *see* a tomb. They go to *see* because that's what Jesus' followers do. The angel invites them to *see* where he lay and instructs them to tell the others that they will *see* him in Galilee. The resurrection of Jesus is about *seeing*.

Many of the exegetical elements we have noted in the previous section might become part of the sermon's fabric.

When making connections, we must also note the difference between preaching *resurrection* (no definite article) and preaching *the resurrection of Jesus*. As Wesley Allen observes, there is a difference between the claim, "Christ *is* risen," and, "Jesus *was* risen,"[23] the latter a question of history and the former a matter of the community's ongoing faith journey. In addition to exposition, the power of story will be crucial. Once again, the text-segment's own form testifies to the power of story.

Raised from the Dead: Resurrection Stories

Overcoming death's sting is one aspect of the story, to be sure. Even today, I received an e-mail about the death of a friend's father and a memorial service this week. Those who confess in creedal language that we believe in "the resurrection from the dead" know we are saying more than something that happened to Jesus. Resurrection applies to us as well.

Edmund Steimle, who taught preaching at Union Theological Seminary in New York, lost his wife on a Saturday before Easter Sunday. Listen to his description of believing in resurrection:

> I found myself the next day seated in the pew of my church on Easter Sunday, a church full of Easter lilies and a brass choir and a springtime congregation singing the "Alleluia's," and they stuck in my throat. I couldn't sing them. I did not believe in the resurrection, not that day, not with what had happened to me. I put down the hymn book. But as I listened to the congregation sing, I realized, "I don't have to believe in the resurrection today. They are believing in the resurrection for me until I can believe in it again for myself."[24]

But death's defeat is not the only message of the resurrection—not hardly. In her memoir, *Memories of God,* Roberta Bondi shares part of her encounter with resurrection. She confesses that growing up she always understood the crucifixion better than the resurrection. It wasn't just the difficulty in believing someone could come back to life, but she related better to Jesus' death. She knew it was something she deserved. As a little child, she longed to be good, to please all of the grown-ups in her world. Her father was an especially demanding person who expected perfection, a perfection that no matter how hard she tried, she knew would never come.

In school she tried to please her teachers, but her anxiety level only made learning that much harder. She struggled with the multiplication tables and, most of all, her self-esteem. She would forget her money for school projects. Her father called her "an underachiever." She looked in the mirror at plain brown pigtails, glasses, and a skinny body. As a ten-year-old she once found herself looking at a rock in the yard and starting to cry as she imagined herself as that rock, alone and silent. Jesus' death seemed to make sense. It gave her a reason to be depressed.

Her parents eventually divorced, something she considered her fault. After graduating from high school, she married and soon discovered that not only was she a miserable daughter, but a poor excuse for a wife. She became a seminary professor and tried to be good at that, while also trying to be a good mother to the two children she had birthed. Later, she divorced and remarried. By the time she was forty-seven her depression became severe. She hit bottom on the Friday afternoon before the Saturday night party to celebrate her tenth wedding anniversary. Her second husband and she had been married ten years earlier on Easter Sunday, a beautiful spring day smelling of dogwoods and azaleas.

Here she was, ten years later, trying desperately to celebrate their anniversary, but terribly depressed. She sank down into a tall red chair and cried to God of how she had failed at everything. Then something happened. How long she sat there she has no idea. But she fell asleep, then suddenly awoke with words from the Roman Catholic Mass going through her head: "The joy of the Resurrection renews the whole world." She had heard the words before, but for the first time every cell in her body knew they were true, true for her. It wasn't that she never battled depression again, but these words brought new life, "The joy of the Resurrection renews the whole world." She felt drunk with joy. "The joy of the Resurrection renews the whole world."[25]

Or think about Rome's attempt to silence Jesus. I think about the legacy of Martin Luther King Jr., who spoke against the empire of racism in his many sermons, but especially the one delivered to the nation with its familiar refrain, "I have a dream." As is well known, his life was cut short by a cruel and senseless assassination at the Lorraine Motel in Memphis. A few years ago the Academy of Homiletics met in Memphis, and together we toured the Civil Rights Museum attached to the old motel. Black and white, male and female, gay and straight, we toured together and took it in, mostly in reverential silence. For me personally, something that occurred just outside the museum was as powerful as anything inside. In front of the motel's infamous balcony, on a plaque embedded in stone, was one line from Scripture, a most surprising text from Genesis: "Behold, here cometh the dreamer. Come now, let us kill him… and see what becomes of his dreams" (37:20). The resurrection overcomes the powers of darkness.

A Theological Caveat

While stories abound about the power of resurrection over death, scholars are quick to note the passive voice in the gospel account: "He *has been* raised from the dead" (28:7). Resurrection is the work of God, and any stories that seem to imply we can overcome obstacles and the like only serve to cheapen the gospel. We do not overcome death, the empire, or our fears by simply trying harder. No, we live into the truth of what God has done in Christ.

Sermon Possibilities

On this Easter Sunday, here are some preaching possibilities:
- Life Overcomes Death
- Victory over the Empire
- Be Not Afraid

A Sermon Sampler

O. Wesley Allen Jr., "Spontaneous Worship," in his *Preaching Resurrection* (St. Louis: Chalice Press, 2000), 59–65.

J. Scott Barker, "Easter Terror," in *Preaching through the Year of Matthew: Sermons that Work*, vol. 10, ed. Roger Alling and David J. Schlafer (Harrisburg, Pa.: Morehouse Publishing, 2001), 52–57.

CHAPTER 8

Matthew 28:16–20

Jesus Commissions His Followers

Locating the Sermon

Trinity Sunday (Year A)

Even if we have preached the lectionary gospel reading every Sunday from the beginning of Lent to the present, it has been some time since we preached from Matthew's account. On Easter Sunday the story of the resurrection comes from Matthew, but now for eight consecutive weeks Luke and John have taken center stage. This lack of a context presents something of a problem for linking the resurrection with the commissioning, which Matthew clearly wants to stress. Added to this, Matthew's commissioning story is read as part of Trinity Sunday, one of those rare moments in the Christian year that focuses upon an isolated doctrine instead of a narrative.

Before we explore how to preach this final passage in Matthew's gospel, we will consider its interpretation. As with so many other passages we have studied, there are many points of entry and exit.

Understanding the Passage

One cannot overemphasize the importance of a good ending for any story. As demonstrated by the gospel of Mark's longer addition (16:9–20), a narrative without an appropriate ending is just begging for someone to pen a conclusion. Matthew, with a creative and insightful flare, composes a conclusion in the last five verses of his gospel that ties together the themes, plots, characters, and theology of the previous twenty-eight chapters. While it is an ending that builds on all that has gone before, it also propels a reader and interpreter into a purposeful future beyond the pages of the gospel. This forward-looking impetus has helped make 28:16–20 one of the most recognized endings in the New Testament, and provided it the label of the "great commission."

How the Evangelist Crafted the Text-segment

This last scene in Matthew between Jesus and his disciples continues a literary strategy that the author has followed throughout his gospel: it is filled with echoes from the Hebrew Scriptures. Just as Jesus' birth at the beginning of Matthew imitates the birth of Moses, now at the completion of the gospel the ending story of Jesus is reminiscent of the ending of Moses' life.[1] As Moses' life in Deuteronomy 31—34 entered its final stage, it centered around commissioning. In these chapters are phrases that provide a hauntingly familiar refrain found also in Matthew's gospel: "When Moses had finished speaking all these words to all Israel, he said to them..." (Deut. 31:1–2a); "When Jesus had finished saying all these things, he said to his disciples..." (Mt. 26:1). It is not just the similarity in wording between Moses and Jesus that draws one's attention from Matthew to these last chapters in Deuteronomy; it is also the content of these Moses' words compared to Jesus' words found in Matthew 28. These words express poignant commissions: one is delivered by a man about to die and the other by a man newly risen from the dead.

Moses' commission to Joshua provides instructions about teaching his words, that is, commandments, to the people of Israel (Deut. 32:46). In this commission, readers learn that Joshua is poised to lead the Israelites into a foreign (Gentile) land (Deut. 31:3–4). Even though Moses leaves behind the community of Israel as he sets out for Moab and Mount Nebo, his presence was still with Joshua "because Moses had laid his hands on him" (Deut. 34:9). The continuing presence of the Lord with Israel is also inscribed within Moses' commission. Joshua is given assurance that it is "the Lord your God who goes with you" (Deut. 31:6).

A sensitive reader of the Bible with an eye trained toward intertextuality can easily capture the parallels between the scene of Moses with Joshua and Jesus with his disciples. Jesus' disciples are instructed to go out among the Gentiles—in other words, into a foreign land—and to teach Jesus' commandments as they are going (Mt. 28:19). Also, the disciples are given assurance that the presence of Jesus will be with them always (Mt. 28:20). While the parallels are significant, so also are the differences. One important difference is that Moses' commission anticipated violence and bloodshed with the destruction of the nations (Deut. 31:3-4). Jesus commissioned his disciples, however, not to destroy the nations, but to baptize, teach, and disciple the nations.

The commission Jesus presents to his disciples follows a literary form frequently found in the Hebrew Scriptures, and its form is repeated in numerous New Testament commissioning stories.[2] Commissioning stories usually have set patterns with stock elements.[3] Matthew 28:16–20 seems to follow closely a typical commissioning form, with only a few exceptions: Introduction (v. 16), Confrontation (v. 17a), Reaction (v. 17b), Protest (v. 17c), Commission (vv. 18–20a), and Reassurance (v. 20b). One difference is that Matthew has compacted the confrontation, reaction, and protest into a single and brief description. Also, an interpreter might question the element of "protest" from the recipients of the commission, the disciples.

The disciples themselves never utter a single word in this commission narrative. The reader of the gospel is left instead with the echo of Jesus' words about a divinely ordained task centered on mission.

N.T. Wright makes a keen observation about the early Christian movement and its expansion:

> The single most striking thing about early Christianity is its speed of growth. In AD 25 there is no such thing as Christianity: merely a young hermit in the Judaean wilderness, and his somewhat younger cousin who dreams dreams and sees visions. By AD 125 the Roman emperor has established an official policy in relation to punishment of Christians... Why then did early Christianity spread? Because early Christians believed that what they had found to be true was true for the whole world. The impetus to mission sprang from the very heart of the early Christian conviction.[4]

Early Christianity praxis was characterized by mission, and Matthew 28:16–20 was (and is) a *crux interpretum* for Christian mission. A closer look at the missional imperative in this commission, however, reveals some surprising insights beyond the typical evangelism impetus usually associated with these verses.

One surprise in this commission is the focusing of discipleship upon the Gentiles. This focus may be obscured, however, because the NRSV and most other translations use the word *nations* instead of *Gentiles* for the Greek word *ethne* (Mt. 28:19). Interestingly, in the NRSV every reference to *ethne* in Matthew 1—20 is translated as "Gentiles," but from chapters 21-28, the translators chose to use the word *nations*. Perhaps the venerable and well-memorized verses of the great commission from the *King James Version* influenced how translators approached *ethne*.

To read verse 19 as a commission to teach, baptize, and disciple Gentiles, however, presents an interpreter with a startling perspective. This is especially true since Matthew frequently, but not always, presents Gentiles in a negative light. Matthew, for example, notes that Gentiles do not know how to pray with sincerity (6:7) and seek only for the objects of desire in this world (6:32). They are the ones who will mock, scourge, and crucify the Son of Man (20:19); and they serve as a negative model for servanthood (20:25–26). Perhaps what is most surprising is that Jesus has previously given his disciples in 10:5 a commission that is in sharp contrast to the "great commission" of chapter 28. Perhaps 10:5 should be called the "Noncommission to Gentiles," since Jesus sends out the Twelve with a commission to "Go nowhere among the Gentiles…" With a focus on Gentiles in the commission of 28:16–20, the author seems to reflect an inclusiveness that only subtly has been presented throughout the gospel but which reaches an explicit climax in these words of the risen Lord.

When considered in relationship to the whole gospel context, this climactic commission for seeking after Gentiles is an example of Matthew's brilliant compositional irony. Consider that Matthew begins his gospel with Gentiles (the stargazers, *magoi*) in 2:1 seeking a Judean, and he ends his gospel with Judeans seeking Gentiles. This irony is highlighted by King Herod's commission to the stargazers to "Go and search diligently for the child; and when you have found him, bring me word so that I may also go and pay him homage" (2:8). Jesus' royal commission for his Judean disciples to seek Gentiles uses the same verbal forms (a participle, "while going," followed by an imperative) as Herod's royal commission for Gentiles to seek a Judean child. It must have been a delightfully delicious drop of ink onto papyrus as Matthew portrayed Jesus, now the resurrected Lord, sending out his disciples on a royal commission to seek Gentiles.

While the "great commission" has typically focused almost exclusively on mission-evangelism, a closer reading of the overall context of Matthew once again can surprise an interpreter. The commission is not just to baptize, but also to teach obedience in all that Jesus commanded (28:20). What would be the content of the commandments that Jesus provided? The reference could be to the numerous teachings of Jesus as found in Matthew, such as the Sermon on Mount. These teachings embrace a radical ethic for living out the reign of God/heaven. So the commission emphasis is not just or only about getting folks *into* the reign of God/heaven, but about *how one lives* in the now of the reign of God/heaven.

That this focus may be primary for the author is supported by the closing words of Jesus' commission to his disciples: "I am with you always, to the end of the age" (28:20). These words are typically taken as a type of security blanket in which disciples then and now can wrap themselves. However, they may also be a challenge and warning. A sensitive reader of Matthew's gospel will recall only three chapters previous, in the story of the sheep and goats (Mt. 25:31–46), that Jesus indicated divine presence might be encountered in unexpected ways. The words uttered by the King/Son of Man to the incredulous goats-people on the left hand are stinging words: "Truly I tell you, just as you did not do it to one of the least of these, you did not do it to me" (25:45). Jesus, Emmanuel, is with us, but in the form of the naked, poor, hungry, thirsty, and ill-clothed. The "great commission" is a "great challenge." It is an ethical challenge thrust upon the disciples to see those around them and to recognize them as the presence of Christ in their midst. As Daniel Patte succinctly notes:

> By observing all that he [Jesus] has commanded them, they [the disciples] will indeed show mercy and compassion for the poor and consequently be in the presence of Jesus; it is to Jesus that they show compassion. Jesus will not be with them in his body (as he was during his ministry), but he will always be with them since "you always have the poor with you" (26:11).[5]

What the Text-segment Meant to the Community

The appearance of Jesus and his delivery of a commission to the disciples may seem on an initial reading to be disconnected from the previous narratives in Matthew 28:1–15, especially the rumor story about the stolen body in verses 11–15. The literary artistry and theological astuteness of Matthew, however, is clearly evident.

In chapter 28, the first appearance of the risen Jesus is not to the male disciples, but to the faithful women disciples (vv. 9–10). Like most positive characters in Matthew's gospel (Mary, Joseph, the disciples in the commission), the women do not speak a word. Instead, the focus remains on Jesus and his words: "Do not be afraid; go and tell my brothers to go to Galilee; there they will see me" (v. 10). The author connected this story with 28:16–20 by highlighting that the eleven disciples went to Galilee to a prearranged place on a mountain that Jesus had designated (v. 16). The women demonstrated they were both faithful and righteous by fulfilling their personal commission to tell the disciples about the rendezvous with the risen Jesus. One other aspect of the women's encounter with Jesus is also paralleled by the one with the male disciples: both groups, when they first encounter Jesus, worship him (v. 9, v. 17).

In a sense, the commission stories of the women and men form a frame around verses 11–15 about the plan the priests and elders devised to disperse a rumor that the disciples had stolen Jesus' body. No doubt the author added this story as a part of an apologetic explanation because of rumors still circulating that the body of Jesus had been stolen. The juxtaposition of this narrative with the commission, however, is very suggestive. The author begins the commission narrative of 28:16–20 with the Greek word *de,* which is a conjunction of contrast. This Greek word is typically translated as "and" or "but." While many translations use a transitional word such as *then* (*now* in the NRSV), it certainly could be appropriate here to begin this section with, "*But* the eleven went to Galilee, to the mountain to which Jesus had directed them" (v. 16). The contrast between the stories and actions could not be greater. The disciples were not taken in by false stories, *but* accepted the truthful witness of the women and acted upon the witness by making their way to Galilee and the mountain Jesus designated. Matthew subtly places before readers a choice of purchased and perjured witness versus authentic and truthful witness.

Matthew sets the initial scene in 28:16 quickly with the presence of eleven disciples. The number eleven brings to mind both the defection and demise of Judas (Mt. 27:3–10). The mountain to which Jesus had directed the disciples is not named, and its exact location is unnecessary from a literary perspective. More important is that for Matthew big events take place on mountains. A reader knows from previous chapters that if a rendezvous takes place on a mountain, it will be a significant and transformative event for those involved. This important event, interestingly, is taking place in a location remote from the power center of Jerusalem and Mount Zion.[6] This geographical pointer signifies that the actions of the disciples will be moving out from a different center than Jerusalem. Galilee is an appropriate location for giving a commission directed toward seeking Gentiles, since it historically carried the label of "Galilee of the Gentiles" (Isa. 9:1 and 1 Mac. 5:15).

In verse 17, the disciples encounter the risen Jesus for the first time. In this encounter, they have two different yet simultaneous responses: they worshiped; they doubted. The juxtaposition of worship and doubt leaves a reader with an interpretative dilemma. How is it possible to worship and doubt at the same time? Can these two seemingly opposite responses coexist? For Matthew, doubt and worship are not strange companions. Previously in the narrative of the boat in the storm, the disciples also demonstrated the twin characteristics of worship and doubt (14:31–33). Mark Allan Powell says that the "church for Matthew is a community of worshiping doubters, a gathering of people of little faith pooling their mustard seeds together, ready to use those seeds, which seem so insignificant, to move mountains."[7] From Matthew's perspective, doubt seems to be a part of the DNA of humanity, but the presence of the Lord allows for the existence within individuals of a germ of faith that can express itself in worship.

For the disciples to embrace Jesus in worship has implications that are sometimes overlooked. From the perspective of Roman imperial theology, worship was due to the gods/goddesses and also to the deified emperors. This worship would guarantee the continuing existence, stability, and prosperity of the Empire. So, for example, emperor Tiberius (14–37 C.E.), emperor during the time of Jesus, could mint coins with the inscription DIVVS AVGVSTVS PATER (Divine Augustus Father) and have temples erected in Augustus's honor. In Judea, Herod the Great erected three temples for the worship of Rome and Augustus.[8] One was located in Caesarea Philippi, an area in which Jesus traveled (Mt. 16:13–20). To worship and give allegiance to Jesus constituted an act of rebellion against the Roman Empire. Worship is never an ambiguous act; it is always fraught with political and religious meaning.

Before Jesus gave the commission to his disciples, he revealed, "All authority...has been given to me" (28:18). This passive construction helps an interpreter realize the source of Jesus' authority is ultimately God. As Matthew brings this gospel to its conclusion, he wants it to end on a theocentric note. God is the one who from the beginning, even as represented in the genealogy, has been involved in bringing about all that has happened.

With Jesus' authority from God, he commissions the disciples to be involved in three distinct directives. Often the first directive is highlighted as the imperative to "go," but actually this Greek word is not an imperative but a participle. It can easily be translated "as you are going." It implies that the essence of the Christian life is a pilgrimage. Clarence Jordan, in his *Cotton Patch* translation, puts it this way, "As you travel..."[9] Being rooted to (and rotting in) one spot was not an option for disciples who were commissioned for God's project in the world.

In the process of going, three responsibilities were laid upon the disciples: to disciple the Gentiles, to baptize, and to teach. The core of discipleship has been illustrated throughout Matthew's gospel by Jesus' life. George Montague summarizes well the essence of Matthean discipleship:

> To be a disciple is to follow Jesus, to share his life-style and his table, to listen to his word, accept it and live by it, to share his mission, to accompany him through the storm, to learn how to live in the community with disciples, to forgive and be reconciled, to bear public witness to Jesus, and finally to make other disciples.[10]

The commission to the disciples also indicates that those coming into discipleship will need to participate in the baptismal experience. Baptism would be the tangible ritual for those early followers leaving one community to experience being reincorporated back into a new community. For those leaving ethnic groups or families, the waters of the baptismal pool become thicker than blood. Baptism for Matthew is the experienced ritual that demonstrates the truth Jesus spoke in Matthew 12:49b–50: "Here are my mother and my brothers! For whoever does the will of my Father in heaven is my brother and sister and mother."

The baptism ritual is specifically experienced in the name of the "Father and of the Son and of the Holy Spirit" (Mt. 28:19). Some scholars understand this advanced Trinitarian formula as a reflection from the author's day versus the day of Jesus. Perhaps this is true, since often in the early church, at least as described by the author of Luke-Acts, baptism was done in the name of Jesus (Acts 2:38; 10:48). The emphasis upon the Holy Spirit, however, is not out of place. Matthew begins his gospel with the coming of the Holy Spirit upon Mary (1:18, 20), so it is not strange that the Spirit finds its way into the closing verses of this gospel.

The last responsibility given to the disciples is that of teaching. This teaching commission is something new for the disciples.[11] When the disciples were commissioned earlier, in Matthew 10:7–8, they were told to preach, heal, and cast out demons, but absent is teaching. Teaching throughout the gospel of Matthew has been the exclusive responsibility of Jesus. The five teaching sections in Matthew are monuments to Jesus' rabbinic vocation. Now this mantle has been passed to the disciples, and the words of Jesus are to live on in the voices of the disciples.

Preaching the Passage

The Familiar and Unfamiliar

Although there are many ways to express what we attempt when we preach each week, one way is to recognize that what happened in the text back then still happens today and that what happens now is sacred as well. Or, in other words, Christ still commissions his church; and these modern-day encounters on his behalf are as meaningful as any first-century incident of evangelism. Or, to put it even more bluntly, the commission given on the mountain in Galilee continues to the present, even if the task is now undertaken by more than the eleven apostles.

At first glance, commissioning stories may seem quite foreign to our experience. None of us has ever been summoned to a mountain where the resurrected Jesus sent us forth to change the world, at least not literally. The form of a commissioning story itself, however, may be more common than we think. As New Testament scholars James Bailey and Lyle Vander Broek note, there are two common elements in these stories: the actual commissioning (always by a higher authority) and the reassurance (to overcome any anticipated resistance).[12] Contemporary analogies, which admittedly often break down, might offer some assistance. Think about coaches and teachers who insisted upon us attempting a task that seemed out of reach, but who assured us they would be there to help. Or think about a parent who ran alongside our bicycle when, for the first time without training wheels, we took to the sidewalks.

Still, some elements in the text-segment are not only foreign to our contemporary experience but also might go largely unnoticed by most churchgoers. As we noted in the earlier part of this chapter, those with a trained eye can easily recognize the parallels between Jesus and Moses. But what about those whose eyes aren't so trained? Once again we preachers face the decision of how much exegetical material to include in the sermon. Is what interests the preacher what should also interest listeners? If we answer negatively, then what about those persons in church who long to know more of the Bible?

For example, Herod's commission to the stargazers parallels Jesus' final commission to his disciples. Should that be included in our sermons? The list goes on and on. One guideline that might prove helpful is to recall the purpose of the sermon. Thomas Long and many other fine homileticians have claimed for decades now that sermons should be cohesive enough that their purpose can be clearly stated in one rather simple sentence—what Long calls a focus statement.[13] If the focus of our sermon includes a contrast of the ways of Jesus versus those of empire, then the answer may well be, "Yes, include the Herod/Jesus contrast." If the focus points in another direction, then the answer may well be, "No."

The same would be true with regards to Matthew's use of Mark. The "great commission" is a very different ending than Mark's "great omission," in which the witnesses of the resurrection fled in terror and said nothing to anyone. How the New Testament canon came to be is a fascinating topic, one currently creating quite a buzz among many churchgoers, especially in light of the Dead Sea Scrolls, the Nag Hammadi library, and books such as *The Gospel of Judas*. Not every "buzz" need be included in every sermon, although some should. Ultimately, preachers should always know more about a text than is shared in the actual sermon. Besides, some material will be more appropriate the next time we preach this passage.

Making Connections

Most preachers are familiar with the so-called "seven last words of Jesus," whereas Shane Stanford considers the "seven next words" of Jesus.[14] In Matthew's account, if one includes the message of the angel at the empty tomb, the first words would be, "Do not be afraid," even prior to the good news, "He has been raised." Similarly, Jesus' first words after his resurrection are "Greetings" (28:9) and then "Do not be afraid" (28:10). A few verses later are these words of commissioning. No doubt the two should be linked; overcoming our fear is prerequisite to our being commissioned to change the world. As we observed earlier, commission stories always include or assume a protest on the part of those being sent. In this case, we are told some doubted. Any sermon that dares to continue the challenge Jesus first gave will have to acknowledge the fear and doubts of listeners.

Preachers might wish to consider another strategy, the indicative approach. Typically preachers approach passages like the so-called "great commission" from an imperative slant. If Jesus commissioned his followers, we as preachers will do the same, recognizing, of course, that we are not Jesus but rather included among those followers. That's the imperative approach, how things *should* be.

The indicative, how things *are,* can also work quite well. Fred Craddock uses the indicative quite effectively in a sermon on this passage. He tells about going to see *Star Wars, Episode I: The Phantom Menace* with his grandsons. They, of course, had already seen episodes 4, 5, and 6; he had not. They finally explained to him that what they were watching was the prequel to the later episodes. Craddock notes:

> There are churches everywhere, grand cathedrals that take your breath away. Beautiful brick and stone and wood buildings, cinder block buildings, too. Simple, inexpensive grass huts, igloos, brush arbors. Everywhere in the world, somebody is reading the Bible and worshiping God and learning about Jesus. That's the sequel.[15]

He then adds, "But what's the *prequel?* Our text is the prequel."[16] Playing off such an analogy, the preacher might tell any number of stories from our day, the sequel to this ancient commission.

Commissioning Stories

Just about any contemporary story in which God is shown to be at work could be used as an example of how the commissioning continues to go forth. I think of the story a minister shared years ago with some of us at a preaching workshop I was leading in Wyoming. The minister's name was Whelan, and sitting over lunch he shared with the group about his grandfather, who had come to America in the early 1900s. His grandfather was a rugged man, self-sufficient and proud, a miner. He'd come over from Europe and was determined to make a decent living for his family. He was a Christian man but didn't care for the Catholics in that community, not even the ones he worked with all those years in the mines. He didn't see the contradiction in being Christian and being prejudiced against Catholics.

Then something happened! In a mining accident he lost one of his legs just below the knee. He couldn't work anymore, couldn't care for his family. And yet nearly every day baskets of food would appear on the doorstep—from the Catholics. In fact, when it came time to get a prosthetic leg, a costly $300 in 1913, the Catholics there raised most of the money. After including the minister's story about his father in a sermon, I asked the congregation, "Do you know your church history? Do you know where Catholics come from? Same place we do: they come from this mountain in Matthew 28!" The story functions as sequel to this prequel commission.

Chloe Breyer's book *The Close* is full of fascinating stories, all of them sequels to the great commission in a way. Breyer is the daughter of Supreme Court justice Stephen Breyer, but the book is not about that at all. No, it's the story of her journey through seminary, including rich stories about all the people she meets there. In a way, it is the story of us all, seminarian or not. She tells about a former Texas rancher named Bransford who had enrolled in the seminary. In addition to raising cattle, he spoke several dialects of Chinese and had, for seven years of his life, walked across China "making disciples." In each village he would enter the marketplace and strike up a conversation with the oldest man he could find. Once the crowds gathered around him, curious about this foreigner talking with the wisest man in the village, and after they had repeatedly asked him what he wanted, only then would he begin to speak about the gospel. That, too, is a sequel to the great commission prequel in Matthew 28.[17]

Sermon Possibilities

This last text-segment in Matthew's gospel lends itself to at least these three options:
- Making Disciples in Every Place Today
- The Christ Who Promises to Be with Us
- The Church as Sequel to Christ's Great Commission

A Sermon Sampler

Three gifted preachers offer three distinct approaches to preaching this passage:

Fred B. Craddock, "What God Wants This Church to Do," in *The Cherry Log Sermons* (Louisville: Westminster John Knox Press, 2001), 42–47.

Anna Carter Florence, "From Beginning to End," *Pulpit Digest* (March/April 1996): 24–28.

William H. Willimon, "A Trinitarian God," *Pulpit Resource* 30 (April/May/June 2002): 34–36.

Notes

Introduction

[1]Harvey Cox, *Common Prayers: Faith, Family, and a Christian's Journey through the Jewish Year* (Boston: Houghton Mifflin, 2001), 161. Emphasis his.

[2]Stephen Fowl, *Engaging Scripture: A Model for Theological Interpretation* (Malden, Mass.: Blackwell, 1998); Mary H. Schertz and Perry B. Yoder, *Seeing the Text: Exegesis for Students of Greek and Hebrew* (Nashville: Abingdon Press, 2001).

[3]Fred B. Craddock, *Preaching* (Nashville: Abingdon Press , 1985), 84–85.

[4]Bruce Malina, "The Bible: Witness or Warrant: Reflections on Daniel Patte's *Ethics of Biblical Interpretation*," *Biblical Theology Bulletin* 26 (Summer 1996): 84.

[5]David M. May, "'Drawn from Nature or Common Life': Social and Cultural Reading Strategies for the Parables," *Review and Expositor* 94 (Spring 1997): 199.

[6]C. Clifton Black, *The Rhetoric of the Gospel: Theological Artistry in the Gospel and Acts* (St. Louis: Chalice Press, 2001), 22.

[7]Thomas G. Long, *Preaching and the Literary Forms of the Bible* (Philadelphia: Fortress Press, 1989), 12. Emphases his.

[8]For example, see James L. Bailey and Lyle D. Vander Broek, *Literary Forms in the New Testament: A Handbook* (Louisville: Westminster/John Knox Press, 1992); and Mike Graves, *The Sermon as Symphony: Preaching the Literary Forms of the New Testament* (Valley Forge, Pa.: Judson Press, 1997).

[9]Saint Augustine, *On Christian Teaching*, Book IV, trans. R.P.H. Green (Oxford: Oxford University Press, 1997), 117.

[10]In the case of Matthew, for example, see M. Eugene Boring, *Matthew* in *New Interpreter's Bible*, vol. 8 (Nashville: Abingdon Press, 1995); Warren Carter, *Matthew and the Margins: A Sociopolitical and Religious Reading* (Maryknoll, N.Y.: Orbis, 2001); Douglas R.A. Hare, *Matthew* in *Interpretation* (Louisville: John Knox Press, 1993); and Thomas G. Long, *Matthew* in *Westminster Bible Companion* (Louisville: Westminster John Knox Press, 1997), all of which we have found most helpful. See the Additional Resources for these homiletical commentaries and other sources consulted.

Chapter 1: Matthew 2:13–23

[1]Although the authorship is actually unknown, we have opted for language the church has adopted over the years. This practice probably makes the most sense when preaching as well.

[2]See James L. Bailey and Lyle D. Vander Broek, *Literary Forms in the New Testament: A Handbook* (Louisville: Westminster/John Knox Press, 1992), 49–54 and 178–83.

[3]Richard J. Erickson, "Divine Injustice?: Matthew's Narrative Strategy and the Slaughter of the Innocents (Mt. 2.13-23)," *Journal of the Study of the New Testament* 64 (1996): 18.

[4]Bruce J. Malina and Jerome H. Neyrey, *Calling Jesus Names: The Social Value of Labels in Matthew* (Sonoma, Calif.: Polebridge, 1988), 117.

[5]Marcus Borg, *Meeting Jesus Again for the First Time: The Historical Jesus and the Heart of Contemporary Faith* (New York: HarperSanFrancisco, 1995), 121–33. Borg also identifies "the priestly story" (an overarching meta-narrative in which sins must be atoned for) as a third macro-story, one that unfortunately has dominated modern-day Christianity.

[6]Harry Emerson Fosdick, "What Is the Matter with Preaching?" *Harpers Magazine* (July 1928): 133–41.

[7]Thomas H. Troeger, *Imagining a Sermon* (Nashville: Abingdon Press, 1990), 62–63.

[8]Patrick J. Willson, "The Massacre of Innocence," *Pulpit Digest* (January/February 1999): 71.

[9]Jonathan Kozol, *Amazing Grace: The Lives of Children and the Conscience of a Nation* (New York: HarperPerennial, 1996), 3.

[10]Ibid., 6.

[11]Ewa Zadrzynska, *The Peaceable Kingdom* (Boca Raton, Fla.: M. M. Art Books, 1994).

[12]Among the most helpful are two volumes by Eugene L. Lowry, *The Homiletical Plot: The Sermon as Narrative Art Form,* exp. ed. (Louisville: Westminster John Knox Press, 2001), and *How to Preach a Parable: Designs for Narrative Sermons* (Nashville: Abingdon Press, 1989).

[13]Jon M. Walton, "In the Days of Herod the King," *Pulpit Digest* (November/December 1993): 38.

[14]M. Eugene Boring, *Matthew* in *New Interpreter's Bible,* vol. 8 (Nashville: Abingdon Press, 1995), 150.

[15]Thomas G. Long, "Foreword," *Journal for Preachers* 1 (Advent 1981): 3.

[16]Fred B. Craddock, "The Hard Side of Epiphany," *Wineskins* 2 (1994): 13. The sermon was part of the *Preaching Today* series first recorded in 1986.

Chapter 2: Matthew 4:1–11

[1]For the definition of an agonistic society, see Bruce Malina, *New Testament World: Insights From Cultural Anthropology,* rev. ed (Louisville: Westminster John Knox Press, 2001), 36.

[2]Ibid., 27–57.

[3]J. Ramsey Michaels, *Servant and Son: Jesus in Parable and Gospel* (Atlanta: John Knox Press, 1981), 47.

[4]Ibid., 48.

[5]Marcus Borg, *Meeting Jesus Again for the First Time: The Historical Jesus and the Heart of Contemporary Faith* (New York: HarperSanFrancisco, 1995), 121–33.

[6]The end of exile motif is a major thesis of N.T. Wright, *Jesus and the Victory of God,* Christian Origins and the Question of God, vol. 2 (Minneapolis: Fortress Press, 1996).

[7]John J. Pilch, "'Beat His Ribs While He is Young' (Sir 30:12): A Window on the Mediterranean World," *Biblical Theology Bulletin* 23 (1993): 101–13.

[8]Warren Carter, *Matthew and the Margins: A Sociopolitical and Religious Reading* (Maryknoll, N.Y.: Orbis, 2000), 110.

[9]See Mike Graves, *The Sermon as Symphony: Preaching the Literary Forms of the New Testament* (Valley Forge, Pa.: Judson Press, 1997), ch. 6.

[10]See Stephen Farris, *Preaching that Matters: The Bible and Our Lives* (Louisville: Westminster John Knox Press, 1998), who discusses the role of analogies in preaching both theologically and practically.

[11]William H. Willimon, "Getting What We Want," *Pulpit Resource* 27 (1999): 33.

[12]Charles L. Campbell, *The Word Before the Powers: An Ethic of Preaching* (Louisville: Westminster John Knox Press, 2002), 46.

[13]Carter, *Matthew and the Margins,* 106.

[14]Nelson Mandela, *Long Walk to Freedom: The Autobiography of Nelson Mandela* (New York: Little, Brown and Co., 1995).

[15]See Graves, *The Sermon as Symphony,* ch. 2, in which a sermon's mood is considered in musical terms.

[16]Paul Scherer, "Let God Be God," in *The Word God Sent* (Grand Rapids: Baker, 1965), 143–44.

[17]Thomas G. Long, "Facing Up to Temptation," in *Whispering the Lyrics: Sermons for Lent and Easter* (Lima, Ohio: CSS, 1995), 17–20. Emphasis his.

[18]Fred B. Craddock, "Tempted to Do Good," in *The Cherry Log Sermons* (Louisville: Westminster John Knox Press, 2001), 16–17.

[19]Willimon, "Getting What We Want," 32.

[20]Stephen King, "The Man in the Black Suit," in *A Celestial Omnibus: Short Fiction on Faith,* ed. J.P. Maney and Tom Hazuka (Boston: Beacon, 1997), 251–71. Another equally wonderful collection is C. Michael Curtis, ed., *God: Stories* (Boston: Houghton Mifflin, 1998).

[21]Fyodor Dostoevsky, *The Brothers Karamazov,* trans. Andrew R. MacAndrew (New York: Bantam, 1970), 297–313. Emphases his.

Chapter 3: Matthew 5:1–12

[1]For the other textual boundary markers, see 11:1; 13:53; and 19:1.

[2]Dale C. Allison Jr. "The Structure of the Sermon on the Mount," *Journal of Biblical Literature,* 103/3 (1987): 423–45.

[3]K.C. Hanson, "How Honorable! How Shameful!: A Cultural Analysis of Matthew's Makarisms and Reproaches," *Semeia* 68 (1996): 83–114. This article is also available online at: www.kchanson.com.

[4]Richard B. Hays, *The Moral Vision of the New Testament: A Contemporary Introduction to New Testament Ethics* (San Francisco: HarperSanFrancisco, 1996), 98.

[5]Hanson, "How Honorable," 94.

[6]Ibid., 104.

[7]William Klassen, "'Love Your Enemies': Some Reflections on the Current Status of Research," in *The Love of Enemy and Nonretaliation in the New Testament,* ed. Willard M. Swartly (Louisville: Westminster/John Knox Press, 1992), 8.

[8]Ibid.

[9]See Alyce McKenzie, *Preaching Biblical Wisdom in a Self-Help Society* (Nashville: Abingdon Press, 2002), 184–85, who offers a healthy alternative to Schuller's approach.

[10]Hanson, "How Honorable," 94.

[11]Warren Carter, *Matthew and the Margins: A Sociopolitical and Religious Reading* (Maryknoll, N.Y.: Orbis, 2000), 130.

[12]Stanley Hauerwas and William H. Willimon, *Resident Aliens* (Nashville: Abingdon Press, 1989), 84.

[13]McKenzie, *Preaching Biblical Wisdom,* 184. See also David Buttrick, *Speaking Jesus: Homiletic Theology and the Sermon on the Mount* (Louisville: Westminster John Knox Press, 2002), 64.

[14]See Mike Graves, "'God of Grace and God of Glory': The Focus of Our Preaching," in *What's the Matter with Preaching Today?: Essays in Honor of the Preaching Ministry of Harry Emerson Fosdick,* ed. Mike Graves (Louisville: Westminster John Knox Press, 2004), 109–25.

[15]Carter, *Matthew and the Margins,* 128–29.

[16]Stanley P. Saunders and Charles L. Campbell, *The Word on the Street: Performing the Scriptures in the Urban Context* (Grand Rapids: Eerdmans, 2000), 87.

[17]Thomas G. Long, *Matthew* in *Westminster Bible Companion* (Louisville: Westminster John Knox Press, 1997), 46–47.

[18]William H. Willimon, "On the Way to a New World," *Pulpit Resource* 30 (January-March 2002): 23.

[19]Alice Walker, "The Welcome Table," in *Faith: Stories,* ed. C. Michael Curtis (Boston: Houghton Mifflin, 2003), 254–58.

[20]Buttrick, *Speaking Jesus,* 75, 77.

[21]Carter, *Matthew and the Margins*, 131. He cites the work of D. Garland, *Reading Matthew: A Literary and Theological Commentary on the First Gospel* (New York: Crossroad, 1995), 54.

[22]Kathleen Norris, *The Cloister Walk* (New York: Riverhead, 1996), 214–15.

[23]Nora Gallagher, *Things Seen and Unseen* (New York: Knopf, 1998), 197.

[24]Barbara Brown Taylor, a sermon in the video series, "The Great Preachers."

[25]Ibid.

Chapter 4: Matthew 14:22–33

[1]For a specific study on Herod Antipas, see Harold W. Hoehner, *Herod Antipas*, Society for New Testament Studies 17 (Cambridge: Cambridge University Press, 1972). For a general perspective on the Herodian dynasty, see Nikos Kokkinos, *The Herodian Dynasty: Origins, Role in Society and Eclipse* (Sheffield: Sheffield Academic Press, 1998).

[2]See our discussion on the birth of Jesus in ch. 1 on Matthew 2:13–23.

[3]The "traditions" would be the oral traditions handed down by various elders from the past. These traditions typically related to issues of purity and were not contained specifically within the laws of Moses.

[4]Warren Carter, *Matthew and the Margins: A Sociopolitical and Religious Reading* (Maryknoll, N.Y.: Orbis, 2000), 311.

[5]For background on the apostle Peter, see Oscar Cullmann, *Peter: Disciple–Apostle–Martyr*, trans. Floyd V. Filson (Philadelphia: Westminster Press, 1953); and Pheme Perkins, *Peter: Apostle for the Whole Church* (Edinburgh: T & T Clark, 2000).

[6]A parallel storm scene with Jesus appearing on the water also occurs in John 6:16–21.

[7]Luke Timothy Johnson, *The Writings of the New Testament: An Interpretation*, rev. ed. (Minneapolis: Fortress Press, 1999), 195–97.

[8]Ibid., 195.

[9]It is a strange phrase to say that Peter "saw the wind" (v. 30). How does one see the wind? One can *experience* the wind, and in that experience Peter is described as being fearful.

[10]Johnson, *The Writings*, 191. The *Birkat-ha-minim* are also called the Eighteen Benedictions.

[11]During a particularly dry season in 1986 when the Sea of Galilee near the ancient city of Magdala (today Migdal) was very low, a boat dated to the first century, probably much like the ones used during Jesus' day, was unearthed. It was 26 feet long, and 7 feet wide and 4 feet deep. John J. Pilch notes that this boat originally had a sail, and there were places for four oarsmen and a tillerman (*The Cultural World of Jesus: Sunday by Sunday, Cycle A* [Collegeville, Minn.: Liturgical Press, 1995], 121).

[12]David E. Garland, *Reading Matthew: A Literary and Theological Commentary on the First Gospel* (New York: Crossroad, 1995), 158. Note the scene in the Acts of the Apostle when Paul, along with 276 other individuals, is on board a ship in the midst of a storm (27:13–44). In the midst of the fourteenth day of fighting the storm, Paul urges all the members of the ship to take food. The author writes, "After he had said this, he took bread; and giving thanks to God in the presence of all, he broke it and began to eat" (27:35).

[13]Frederick Buechner, *Whistling in the Dark: An ABC Theologized* (San Francisco: Harper & Row, 1988), 85–86.

[14]See my chapter on miracle stories in Mike Graves, *The Sermon as Symphony: Preaching the Literary Forms of the New Testament* (Valley Forge, Pa.: Judson Press, 1997), 104–31.

[15]Michael Hough, "For Those Who Trust in God," in *Best Sermons 5*, ed. James W. Cox (San Francisco: HarperSanFrancisco, 1992), 86.

[16]Kathleen Norris, *Amazing Grace: A Vocabulary of Faith* (New York: Riverhead Books, 1998), 120. A version of the sermon I preached was published under the title, "Followed by the Sun: Matthew 14:22–33," in *Review and Expositor* 99 (Winter 2002): 91–96.

[17]Douglas R.A. Hare, *Matthew* in *Interpretation* (Louisville: John Knox Press, 1993), 169.

[18]Carol Marie Norén, "Christ—Beside Us in the Storm," *Pulpit Resource* 27 (July-September 1999): 25.

[19]Thomas C. Foster, *How to Read Literature Like a Professor: A Lively and Entertaining Guide to Reading Between the Lines* (New York: Quill, 2003), 8.

[20]Frederick Buechner, *The Storm* (San Francisco: HarperSanFrancisco, 1998).

[21]Barbara Brown Taylor, *The Seeds of Heaven: Sermons on the Gospel of Matthew* (Louisville: Westminster John Knox Press, 2004), 58.

[22]Ibid.

Chapter 5: Matthew 21:1–11

[1]Paul W. Meyer, "Matthew 21:1–11," *Interpretation* 40, no. 2 (1986): 180–81.

[2]Ibid., 181.

[3]Ibid.

[4]K.C. Hanson and Douglas E. Oakman, *Palestine in the Time of Jesus: Social Structures and Social Conflicts* (Minneapolis: Fortress Press, 1998), 51.

[5]Ibid., 52.

[6]See other observations about the role of mountains in the gospel of Matthew on pp. 32–33, 136.

[7]Warren Carter, *Matthew and the Margins: A Sociopolitical and Religious Reading* (Maryknoll, N.Y.: Orbis, 2001), 415.

[8]The Judean historian Josephus provides an excellent example of how Judean crowds could be divided into two different groups with two different viewpoints. In May of 4 B.C.E., after the death of King Herod and while his sons were in Rome petitioning Caesar Augustus for positions of power, a rebellion broke out during the festival of Pentecost. As recorded by Josephus, the rebellion was caused by outsiders, pilgrims, from "Galilee, from Idumaea, from Jericho, and from Peraea beyond the Jordan" and also "the native population of Judaea itself" (*Jewish Wars*, II, 42). When the Roman legate Varus arrived in Jerusalem with two legions, the rebellious pilgrims fled. The crowd in Jerusalem, however, welcomed the Roman legate and "disclaimed all responsibility for the revolt, asserting that they themselves had never stirred, that the festival had compelled them to admit the crowd, and that they had been rather besieged with the Romans than in league with the rebels" (*Jewish War*, II, 73).

[9]Joachim Jeremias, *Jerusalem in the Time of Jesus* (Philadelphia: Fortress Press, 1969), 83.

[10]William R. Herzog, II, *Prophet and Teacher: An Introduction to the Historical Jesus* (Louisville: Westminster John Knox Press, 2005), 225.

[11]Peter J. Holliday, *Roman Historical Commemoration in the Visual Arts* (Cambridge: Cambridge University Press, 2002), 22.

[12]Ibid., 24.

[13]Walter Wink, "Beyond Just War and Pacificism: Jesus' Nonviolent Way," *Review & Expositor* 89 (1992): 202. See also Walter Wink, *Jesus and Nonviolence: A Third Way*. Facets (Minneapolis: Fortress Press, 2003).

[14]Carter, *Matthew and the Margins*, 413.

[15]Ron Hansen, *A Stay Against Confusion: Essays on Faith and Fiction* (New York: HarperCollins, 2001), xi.

[16]For example, see M. Eugene Boring, *Matthew* in *The New Interpreter's Bible* (Nashville: Abingdon Press, 1995), 403.

[17]Carter, *Matthew and the Margins*, 413.

[18]Anne Lamott, *Plan B: Further Thoughts on Faith* (New York: Riverhead, 2005), 73.

[19]Ibid., 137–38.

Chapter 6: Matthew 25:14–30

[1]Thomas G. Long, *Preaching and the Literary Forms of the Bible* (Philadelphia: Fortress, 1989), 87.

[2]N.T. Wright, *The New Testament and the People of God,* Christian Origins and the Question of God, vol. 1 (Minneapolis: Fortress Press, 1992), 77.

[3]Eduard Schweizer, *The Good News According to Matthew,* trans. David E. Green (Atlanta: John Knox Press, 1975), 480.

[4]For an excellent article on the variety of different approaches to parables, see Charles W. Hedrick, "Prolegomena to Reading Parables: Luke 13:6–9 as a Test Case," *Review & Expositor* 94 (Spring 1997): 179–97. As Hedrick writes, "New Testament scholars do not agree on what a parable is and how it functions—and neither did the canonical evangelists" (p. 179).

[5]C.H. Dodd, *The Parables of the Kingdom* (London: Nisbet & Co., 1953), 16.

[6]David M. May, "'Drawn from Nature or Common Life': Social and Cultural Reading Strategies for the Parables," *Review & Expositor* 94 (Spring 1997): 199.

[7]Richard L. Rohrbaugh, "A Peasant Reading of the Parable of the Talents/Pounds: A Text of Terror?" *Biblical Theology Bulletin* 23, no. 1 (Spring 1993): 35.

[8]Craig S. Keener, *Commentary on the Gospel of Matthew* (Grand Rapids: Eerdmans, 1999), 601, fn 224. Only a few translations attempt to capture the fearfulness in verse 26. In the *Scholars Version* (SV), the master's rebuke is translated as, "You incompetent and timid slave!" (Robert J, Miller, ed., *The Complete Gospels: Annotated Scholars Version* [Sonoma, Calif.: Polebridge, 1992], 105.

[9]William R. Herzog, II, *Parables as Subversive Speech: Jesus as Pedagogue of the Oppressed* (Louisville: Westminster John Knox Press, 1994), 167.

[10]Ibid.

[11]Rohrbaugh, "A Peasant Reading," 38.

[12]Joseph M. Webb and Robert Kysar, *Greek for Preachers* (St. Louis: Chalice Press, 2002), 87–88.

[13]J. Ramsey Michaels, *Servant and Son: Jesus in Parable and Gospel* (Atlanta: John Knox Press, 1981), 102.

[14]Ibid., 106.

[15]For a thorough discussion of what Jesus perceived in his going to the crucifixion, see N.T. Wright, *Jesus and the Victory of God,* Christian Origins and the Question of God, vol. 2 (Minneapolis: Fortress Press, 1996), 553–611.

[16]See Thomas Long's well-known book, *The Witness of Preaching,* which has been revised into a second edition (Louisville: Westminster John Knox Press, 2005), as well as David J. Lose, *Confessing Jesus Christ: Preaching in a Postmodern World* (Grand Rapids: Eerdmans, 2003), especially ch. 6.

[17]Although personal testimony has been debated much by preachers, see Richard L. Thulin, *The "I" of the Sermon: Autobiography in the Pulpit* (Minneapolis: Fortress Press, 1989); and the more recent volume by Anna Carter Florence, *Preaching as Testimony* (Louisville: Westminster John Knox Press, 2007).

[18]Richard A. Jensen, *Preaching Matthew's Gospel* (Lima, Ohio: CSS Publishing, 1998), 217–18.

[19]Long, *The Witness of Preaching*, 204–18. His introduction to the notion of illustrating sermons is also worth considering, since so much of our approach to stories has been influenced by the rationalism of the Enlightenment (see ch. 8).

[20]Ibid., 216.

[21]Joseph Naveh, "The Greek Alphabet: New Evidence," *Biblical Archaeologist* 43 (Winter 1980): 22–25.

[22]The exegetical presuppositions for this sermon are presented in Rohrbaugh, "A Peasant Reading," 32–39.

Chapter 7: Matthew 28:1–10

[1]Dale C. Allison, "Matthew 28:1–10," in *The Lectionary Commentary, Third Readings: The Gospels* (Grand Rapids: Eerdmans, 2001), 154.

[2]Thomas G. Long, *The Senses of Preaching* (Atlanta: John Knox Press, 1988), 41.

[3]The resurrection accounts are found in Mark 16:1–8; Luke 24:1–12; and John 20:1–10.

[4]W.D. Davies and Dale C. Allison, *The Gospel According to Saint Matthew,* The International Critical Commentary, vol. 3 (Edinburgh: T. & T. Clark, 1997), 670.

[5]Anthony J. Saldarini, "Reading Matthew Without Anti-Semitism," in *The Gospel of Matthew in Current Study,* ed. David E. Aune (Grand Rapids: Eerdmans, 2001), 169.

[6]Ibid.

[7]See especially Saldarini's thoughtful suggestions for avoiding anti-Semitism in Matthew, "Reading Matthew Without Anti-Semitism," 182–83.

[8]Craig S. Keener, *A Commentary on the Gospel of Matthew* (Grand Rapids: Eerdmans, 1999), 696.

[9]For the role of Mary Magdalene in the New Testament and tradition, see Holly E. Hearon, *The Mary Magdalene Tradition: Witness and Counter-Witness in Early Christian Communities* (Collegeville, Minn.: Liturgical Press, 2004); and Ann Graham Brock, *Mary Magdalene, The First Apostle: The Struggle for Authority* (Cambridge: Harvard Divinity School, 2003).

[10]Warren Carter, *Matthew and the Margins: A Sociopolitical and Religious Reading* (Maryknoll, N.Y.: Orbis, 2000), 544.

[11]This earthquake is not the first in Matthew's gospel. At the death of Jesus, an earthquake occurs (27:51). It is a fitting climax that at Jesus' resurrection announcement an earthquake also occurs.

[12]Joseph M. Webb and Robert Kysar, *Greek for Preachers* (St. Louis: Chalice Press, 2002), 47.

[13]M. Eugene Boring, *Matthew* in *The New Interpreter's Bible,* vol. 8 (Nashville: Abingdon Press, 1995), 499.

[14]An extensive work on the resurrection is by N.T. Wright, *The Resurrection of the Son of God* (Minneapolis: Fortress Press, 2003). It is good to balance Wright's perspective with Marcus J. Borg, *Jesus: Uncovering the Life Teachings, and Relevance of a Religious Revolutionary* (San Francisco: HarperSanFrancisco, 2006). Especially helpful is the dialogue between Borg and Wright in their book *The Meaning of Jesus: Two Visions* (San Francisco: HarperSanFrancisco, 1999). See "Part IV: 'God Raised Jesus from the Dead,'" 111–42.

[15]Boring, *Matthew,* 500.

[16]Clarence Jordan, *The Cotton Patch Version of Matthew and John* (Chicago: Association Press, 1970), 96.

[17]James Alison, *Raising Abel: The Recovery of the Eschatological Imagination* (New York: Crossroad, 2000), 29.

[18]John Frederick Jansen, *The Resurrection of Jesus Christ in New Testament Theology* (Philadelphia: Westminster Press, 1980), 67.

[19]Donald A. Hagner, *Matthew 14—28* in *Word Biblical Commentary* (Dallas: Word Books, 1995), 867.

[20]Lee Strobel, *The Case for Christ: A Journalist's Personal Investigation of the Evidence for Jesus* (Grand Rapids: Zondervan, 1998).

[21]For a fascinating treatment of resurrection from an apologetic viewpoint of sorts, see William H. Willimon, *Proclamation and Theology* (Nashville: Abingdon Press, 2005), 73–76, and Long, *The Senses of Preaching*, 38-46, both of whom address the strange logic of Paul's resurrection preaching in 1 Corinthians 15.

[22]Carter, *Matthew and the Margins*, 544.

[23]O. Wesley Allen Jr., *Preaching Resurrection* (St. Louis: Chalice Press, 2000), 2. Emphases his.

[24]Edmund Steimle, as quoted in Robert C. Dykstra, *Discovering a Sermon: Personal Pastoral Preaching* (St. Louis: Chalice Press, 2001), 138.

[25]Roberta C. Bondi, *Memories of God: Theological Reflections on a Life* (Nashville: Abingdon Press, 1995), 145-74.

Chapter 8—Matthew 28:16–20

[1]W. D. Davies and Dale C. Allison Jr., *The Gospel According to Saint Matthew,* vol. 3 The International Critical Commentary (Edinburgh: T & T Clark, 1997), 680–84.

[2]Terence Y. Mullins, "New Testament Commission Form, Especially in Luke-Acts," *Journal of Biblical Literature* 95 (1976): 603–14, suggests that there are a total of thirty-seven commissioning narratives in the gospel of Luke and Acts.

[3]James L. Bailey and Lyle D. Vander Broek, *Literary Forms in the New Testament: A Handbook* (Louisville: Westminster/John Knox Press, 1992), 144–47.

[4]N.T. Wright, *The New Testament and the People of God,* Christian Origins and the Question of God, vol. 1 (Minneapolis: Fortress Press, 1992), 359–60.

[5]Daniel Patte, *The Gospel According to Matthew: A Structural Commentary on Matthew's Faith* (Philadelphia: Fortress Press, 1987), 402.

[6]Warren Carter, *Matthew and the Margins: A Sociopolitical and Religious Reading* (Maryknoll, N.Y.: Orbis, 2000), 551.

[7]Mark Allan Powell, *Loving Jesus* (Minneapolis: Fortress Press, 2004), 125.

[8]Peter Richardson, *Herod: King of the Jews and Friend of Romans* (Columbia: University of South Carolina Press, 1996), 184.

[9]Clarence Jordan, *The Cotton Patch Version of Matthew and John* (Chicago: Association Press, 1970), 97.

[10]George T. Montague, S.M., *Companion God: A Cross-Cultural Commentary on the Gospel of Matthew* (New York: Paulist Press, 1989), 327.

[11]Richard A. Edward, "Uncertain Faith: Matthew's Portrait of the Disciples," in *Discipleship in the New Testament,* ed. Fernando F. Segovia (Philadelphia: Fortress Press, 1985), 59.

[12]Bailey and Broek, *Literary Forms in the New Testament,* 144.

[13]Thomas G. Long, *The Witness of Preaching,* 2ᵈ ed. (Louisville: Westminster John Knox Press, 2005), 108–16.

[14]Shane Stanford, *The Seven Next Words of Christ: Finding Hope in the Resurrection Sayings* (Nashville: Abingdon Press, 2006).

[15]Fred B. Craddock, *The Cherry Log Sermons* (Louisville: Westminster John Knox Press, 2001), 43.

[16]Ibid. Emphasis Craddock's.

[17]Chloe Breyer, *The Close: A Young Woman's First Year in Seminary* (New York: Basic, 2000), 20–21.